PHILIP'S

EGYPT

PHILIP'S

EGYPT

PETER STOCKS

PHOTOGRAPHY BY DAVID COULING

ACKNOWLEDGMENTS

TITLE PAGE *At Abu Qirqus near the ancient city of Hermopolis, a fisherman meditates against the eternal background of the Nile.*

A book of this nature would be impossible to accomplish without the generous assistance of various organizations and individuals both in Egypt and in the British Isles.

I am indebted to the Director and staff of the Egyptian Antiquities Organization, the Director and staff of the Egyptian Press Association, Professor Dr Ali Hassan, Dr Aram Y. Churuqian, and Mr Ayman Makhlouf of the Cataract Hotel, Aswan. I am also grateful to Bill Philip, City of Westminster College, for his valued support; Neil Fitzgerald, Photographic Assistant, who braved the long hot summer of 1991 with me; Kate Gohar, Personal Assistant, for keeping me firmly on the tracks; and my editor, Theresa Wright, for her assistance and advice.

The monuments of Egypt are in very real danger of deterioration due, in part, to the large number of tourists who visit them each year. Remember not to climb or touch them and please do not use electronic flash in the tombs as the irreplaceable paintings are dangerously affected by strong light. In this way, generations to come may yet experience the wonder of an ancient land.

David Couling, London 1992

First published by George Philip, 59 Grosvenor Street, London W1X 9DA

British Library Cataloguing in Publication Data

Stocks, Peter
Philip's Egypt
I. title
916.204

ISBN 0-540-01264-5

Page design by Jessica Caws
Printed in Italy

Contents

◆

Mediterranean Sea
N
Rosetta
Damietta
Port Said
Matruh
Alexandria
El Arish
El Alamein
Tanta
El Mansura
Suez Canal
Zagazig
Wadi Natrun
Heliopolis
Suez
SINAI
Giza
MEMPHIS
Cairo
Lake Qarun
Dahshur
Fayyum
Hawarah
Siwah
Beni Suef
Wadi Feran
St Catherine's Monastery
Biba
River Nile
Beni Mazar
Mt Sinai
Bahriyyah
WESTERN DESERT
Minya
Beni Hasan
Ashmunayn
Mallawi
Tell el Amarna
EASTERN DESERT
Manfalut
Red Sea
Asyut
Tahta
Akhmim
Farafrah
Sohag
Girga
DENDERAH
Abydos
NAQADA
WESTERN THEBES
Luxor
Khargah
Esna
Dakhlah
al-Kab
Kom al-Ahmar
Edfu
Gabal Silsilah
Kom Ombo
E G Y P T
Aswan
Lake Nasser
ABU SIMBEL
0 km 200
SUDAN

Introduction

'so many marvellous things'

HERODOTUS, 5TH CENTURY BC

◆

Of all the nations of the world, only Egypt can claim a recorded occupation of the same territory during an unbroken period of 5000 years. Over this vast span of time Egypt has been witness to the rise and fall of a multitude of other powers, from the city states of western Asia to the mighty empires of Persia, Greece and Rome. In Islamic times, the Baghdad Caliphate came and went, followed by its Ottoman Turk successors. Egypt felt the weight of the British Empire at its peak, and outlived that Empire, too. Whether subject to others or master of its own destiny, Egypt has retained a unique national integrity that has entranced, influenced and often absorbed the visitors of five millennia, whether they first came as slaves, like the ancient Hebrews, mercenary soldiers, like the Greeks, merchants, from everywhere around the Mediterranean, or simply as curious travellers from all over the world.

As if to compensate for its cultural complexity, Egypt as a geological entity is relatively uncomplicated. A base of ancient granites and slates is overlaid by later strata of wind-deposited sandstone or marine limestones which in some areas have been compressed into seams of marble. Covering all is a blanket of gravelly sands through which the harder rocks emerge in chains of hills or escarpments or are exposed in depressions formed by wind or water. Through the now arid desolation of the desert the River Nile cuts a way from its two sources in the highlands of Ethiopia and the equatorial African lakes, carrying the nutrients that once were deposited for several kilometres either side of the margins during the annual inundation from August to October. Thus was life made possible along the banks of the Nile on the rich soil scores of metres thick, while canals and dikes brought the whole of the Delta, once a vast marsh, under intensive cultivation. Throughout Egypt's history, most of its population has lived along this narrow strip, sustained by its phenomenal productivity.

MAP OF EYGPT, OPPOSITE
Names in small capital letters refer to historical sites, and names in ordinary type to existing towns.

A hyena is captured and trussed by his keepers in a Giza tomb relief. The animal's submission may symbolize triumph over the agents of chaos, whose domain, like the hyena's, was the desert.

In the Delta, willows and reeds line the canals for many kilometres, surrounding orchards of citruses, apricots and mangoes and fields of cotton, tomatoes, potatoes and other crops; near the great brackish lakes towards the sea, vast stands of reeds and water vegetation hint at the region's prehistoric appearance. Along the Nile brilliant green fields of sprouting rice, sugar-cane or *berseem* (Egyptian clover) are surrounded by groves of date palms, the strangely branched dum palm or giant sycamore figs.

But the desert is never far away: the Sahara covers 95 per cent of Egyptian territory. In prehistoric times it was a vast savannah, and even now shrubs like acacia and tamarisk and hardy herbs survive wherever there is minimal moisture. In certain areas, underground springs have created oases where lush vegetation surrounds large pools; a string of them are found in Egypt's Western Desert. Khargah and Dakhlah, the two closest to the Nile, have always been relatively well populated and under Egyptian jurisdiction; Bahriyyah and Farafrah, further out, were less important. Siwah, close to the Libyan border was always last to feel the power of successive conquerors from the east; despite its isolation it remained important as the site of the oracular Temple of Amun and as a vital staging post on the trans-Saharan caravan trails and, later, pilgrimage routes.

But most of the Sahara is lifeless, covered by shingle or fine gravels: only in central areas such as the Great Sand Sea are there the shifting dunes of fine sand that most people associate with a desert. Yet despite the harsh conditions, the desert has always supported a population of nomads – nowadays Arabs and Berbers, whose precarious existence would be untenable without the camel, so superbly adapted to desert life. Visitors should stock up with petrol and water before travelling in the Sahara, for despite the excellent system of roads the terrain can be treacherous. Warm clothes are necessary, as the temperature, furnace-like by day, can be bitterly cold at night. However, the rewards for travelling in this hostile territory are great: the infinite views and magnificent sunsets; by night the brilliant stars, or the welcome flicker of a distant encampment fire; and, perhaps most of all, the silence.

It is hardly surprising that the desert attracted contemplatives in the early days of Christianity. But for the majority of ancient Egyptians it was an abode of terror where the realm of chaos, personified in the howling sandstorm, came dangerously close to the human world, and for his association with this land the powerful god Seth was abhorred.

The ancient Egyptians were intrigued yet awed by the abundant wildlife of the country, and many creatures were elevated to the status of cults, used as hieroglyphs or incorporated in wall decorations in naturalistic fashion. Plant forms such as lotus, palm and papyrus were models for columns and other architectural details. Although the wildlife of Egypt is still comparatively rich, it is impoverished compared to early historical times. Gone are the symbols of ancient Egypt, lion, hippopotamus and baboon; the sacred ibis and the crocodile have also disappeared, while the two representative plants, the papyrus and blue water lily, are now extremely rare. Most obvious among the fauna are the birds: herons, lapwings, and various stilt-birds and waders can be seen along the Nile, while the turtle dove, the green bee-eater and the white kite inhabit the cities as well as the plains. The desert supports some mammals – camels, hyenas, gerbils and small mice – but reptiles, well adapted to endure the extremes of temperature and lack of water, are far more plentiful.

'Egypt,' wrote the Greek historian Herodotus in 453 BC, 'is, as it were, the gift of the river.' His much-quoted observation was and is quite true, but only up to a point: the Nile's gifts have not always been reliable. Usually a generous mistress, the river could be cruel to her people if the central African rains either failed or fell to excess. Whether the Nile's inundations were withheld or given in over-abundance the result was the most appalling famine – the ever-present fear central to the dream of Joseph as told in both the Old Testament and the Koran. Perhaps the most detailed description of such a disaster was that of the Arab scientist Abd al-Latif al-

Farmers join together in the sugar-cane harvest, an activity involving their entire village. The plant was probably introduced, along with rice, at the time of the 7th-century Arab conquest; both were soon naturalized.

Baghdadi who witnessed two years of famine at the end of the 13th century AD, when hundreds of thousands died; 'many times', he wrote, 'I fled from the sight of such great horror'. The Nile's capriciousness was restrained by the development of dams and barrages from the mid-19th century. The High Dam at Aswan, built in the early 1960s, now controls the river all year round and protects crops from the annual floods, though it has had an adverse effect on the ecology of the area: the silt which was once deposited along the Nile now gathers behind the artificial lake created by the dam, leaving the river banks dangerously prone to erosion.

Herodotus' idea of a 'gift' also failed to acknowledge the bone-breaking efforts of the farmers in producing the bounty from the land. 'These people get their harvest with less labour than anywhere else in the world, 'he wrote: an example of urban attitudes to rural toil that have not changed much from the earliest times to the twentieth century. In fact, then as now many Nile farmers worked 24 hours a day, if a full moon would let them, while the profits of their labours went to others. Throughout Egyptian history the farmer was exploited, abused and bled dry: all the great monuments, in a sense, were built upon his sweating back.

Herodotus' report remains invaluable as the earliest record by a visitor of his impressions of Egypt. He was visiting a country already incredibly ancient: it is somewhat sobering to recall that he is nearer in time to us by some hundred years than he was to the earliest rulers of the 1st Dynasty.

Ancient Egypt has no single written history as Greece and Rome do; what we know has been gleaned from fragmentary sources such as inscriptions or paintings in tombs and temples, and preserved papyri. The following historical summary can only focus on some of the most important people and events. (You will find the chronological table at the end of the book useful for quick reference when you are trying to place the historical sites in context.)

Although prehistoric settlements sites have been excavated throughout the drier areas of the Nile valley, they are unrewarding to the general visitor; many of them have in any case been re-buried by wind-driven sand, the bane of the archaeologist in Egypt. Even the Sphinx has suffered the indignity of periodic covering and exposure. Only as we approach the historical period are more substantial remains evident, at Hierakonpolis and Naqada in the south. Other sites in the Delta or closer to the banks of the Nile have long been obliterated under the silt. We do know, however, that the Nile Valley was cultivated from about 4500 BC, and that there was a difference in lifestyle between the peoples of the Delta and those of 'Upper Egypt' farther upstream.

The political unification of 'Upper' and 'Lower' Egypt happened about 3050 BC. It was a relatively rapid process, although the impetus for it and the exact sequence of events remain uncertain. Unification was preceded by increasing urbanization is Upper Egypt and probably the Delta. But instead of stabilizing at the level of independent city-states, the usual pattern in the Middle East during the next thousand years, the emergent Egyptian leadership soon controlled the vast area from the north coast to Aswan.

Memphis, close to the point where the Nile splits to form its broad delta, became the capital, and the ruler took the title Horus, King of Upper and Lower Egypt. The first ruler, according to tradition, was called Menes; a clear identification of the founder of the unified state with one of the earliest known kings of the 1st Dynasty, Narmer or Aha, remains elusive.

Culturally the Egyptians of this period were a copper-using people with a long-developed pottery tradition and an extraordinary facility for fashioning hard stone, literate in a quickly developing hieroglyphic script. Domestic animals included goats, sheep, cows, pigs and donkeys while they grew a wide range of crops among which were primitive wheat, barley, beans, grapes and figs. Their religion was based on the veneration of animals, plants, inanimate objects or events. The origins of these cults in the various districts of Egypt is obscure, but associations with their original centres persisted throughout the long millennia of the dynastic period. All were absorbed into a national theology and were to accumulate and evolve into an elaborate mythology over the centuries.

In one particular area however, the Egyptians left ample evidence of their beliefs, with their lavish brick and stone monuments for the dead. Kings of the first two dynasties were buried either at Saqqarah near Memphis or at Abydos in the south, both of which have sizeable brick-built tombs. Clearly, ancient Egyptians felt that a ruler needed someone to carry out menial tasks for him in the afterlife: the earliest tombs contained remains of large-scale executions of retainers. Although the practice was soon abandoned, the belief clearly persisted, for later Old Kingdom tombs contained models of servants.

As depicted on funerary fragments, ceremonial was already an essential part of the duties of the ruler. His visible signs of authority were the tall white crown of Upper Egypt and the flat red crown of Lower Egypt – symbolized by the sedge plant for the former and the bee for the latter – and his protectors were the goddesses Nekhbet of Upper Egypt and Wadjet of Lower Egypt. This duality and its signs continued for the remainder of dynastic rule. At least two other gods were worshipped at this time: Horus, the celestial falcon and epitome of divine kingship, whose earthly manifestation was the ruler himself; and Seth, a weird hybrid animal who later played an equivocal role in Egyptian mythology – at least one ruler in the 2nd Dynasty, Peribsen, accepted him as his patron instead of Horus.

OLD KINGDOM (*c* 2695–2160 BC

By this time Egypt already had a complex system of social institutions, all answerable to the king, who controlled much of the wealth produced by copper and turquoise mines in the Sinai, and from trade with the near east and Nubia. Much was spent on funerary architecture, which during the 3rd Dynasty developed rapidly. For his tomb, Zoser, second king of the dynasty, erected an imposing six-storied stone block structure at Saqqarah, the necropolis of Memphis. Surrounding it was a vast rectangular arena set with ceremonial kiosks and platforms obviously designed for elaborate festivities. The design of the whole complex was by tradition credited to his chancellor Imhotep. This vast display of wealth and power encouraged his successors to emulate his triumph, but all their structures remained incomplete.

Sneferu, first king of the 4th Dynasty, built the first true pyramid, a development of Zoser's structure, at Dahshur to the south. In fact he built two: the first, in which the angle of the sides had to be changed to prevent collapse, was apparently unsatisfactory and another was raised nearby. Surrounding the area are the graves of officials, signs of a growing bureaucracy whose tombs proliferated around those of Sneferu's successors: Khufu, builder of the Great Pyramid at Giza, and Khafre, who added the massive Sphinx to his own complex.

Each of these later pyramids has a mortuary temple against the pyramid itself, where the funerary rites were performed, and a causeway leading to a valley temple built for the rites of the cult of the kings, maintained for centuries after their deaths.

The stepped pyramid of Zoser, the first king to build in stone, rises beyond the external wall of the mortuary complex at Saqqarah. Originally the wall enclosed the entire complex, including the pyramid itself.

Sculpted pillars form an integral part of a wall in the precinct of King Zoser at Saqqarah. The stone pillars, erected before 2600 BC, are the oldest in Egypt; their shape probably imitates the papyrus bundles that were used to support less permanent structures.

This was a period of increasing importance of the sun-god Re which culminated during the 5th Dynasty, the rulers of which lavished their wealth on monumental sun temples built near Memphis, each dominated by a huge obelisk (*benben*), symbol of the sun's force. Most complete is that of Nyuserre, first king of the dynasty. Pyramids were still erected, though much diminished in size. The Pyramid Texts, the first coherent evidence of the beliefs of the Egyptians, date from the 5th Dynasty. These were funerary texts inscribed on the interior walls of the Pyramid of Unas, last king of the dynasty, at Saqqarah. As well as being the earliest, they are the most comprehensive and purest collection of ancient Egyptian funerary literature, which was meant to guide the soul of the deceased in his passage through the afterlife. The increasing influence of the highly literate administrators in this period may have been one of the reasons for the decline of royal authority; whatever the cause, after the death of the last king, Pepi II, who is reputed to have reigned for ninety years, central authority collapsed and the succeeding 8th Dynasty controlled only northern Egypt with provincial governors contesting for power in the south.

Sadly little is left of Memphis, city of the god Ptah, which remained the administrative capital of Egypt until the foundation of Alexandria. It lay close to the more recent city of Cairo and its monuments were systematically plundered for building materials. What is left lies buried under the date groves of Mit Rahinah, although archaeologists are gradually revealing the foundations of temples and palaces and the full extent of the vast site. But the Memphis necropolis, which stretches 60 kilometres from north of Giza to Maydum in the south, contains many more visible remains, including the tombs of most of the kings of the 1st-6th dynasties and hundreds of government servants.

The pioneer archaeologist in the central area of Saqqarah was Auguste Mariette (*d* 1881) who in 1850 began the first systematic excavations. Although his methods were crude – he was a great advocate of the benefits of gunpowder in his work – he did discover the Serapeum, the subterranean burial galleries of the bulls who were living symbols of the bull-god Apis. He subsequently excavated dozens of sites throughout Egypt, clearing many of them of the accumulated detritus of centuries, and later formed the Egyptian Museum.

FIRST INTERMEDIATE PERIOD (*c* 2134-2040 BC) AND MIDDLE KINGDOM (2040-1785 BC)

The collapse of the 6th Dynasty was followed by a stormy time of civil war, which culminated in a 10th Dynasty, ruling from Herakleopolis, near the Fayyum, confronting an 11th Dynasty established at Hermonthis (later Thebes, or modern Luxor) in Upper Egypt. Victory went to the latter under Mentuhotpe, who went on

to found of the 12th Dynasty and the unified Middle Kingdom. During this period Nubia (modern Sudan) was conquered under Amenemhet I. The southern city Abydos gained importance as the centre of a hugely popular cult of Osiris.

11th-Dynasty kings were buried at Thebes where Mentuhotpe built a magnificent funerary temple directly abutting the escarpment. Thereafter the capital was moved to It-Tawi, probably on the southern outskirts of Memphis, and the kings returned to burial in pyramids, though built of brick rather than stone. Stability was achieved through the suppression of the independent nomads and the practice of appointing the most competent son of the king as co-ruler. During this period there was considerable activity at the Fayyum, the nearest agricultural territory to the capital. Watered by the great lake Qarun, once called Moeris, the semi-oasis of the Fayyum has always been an area of great productivity. In ancient times, the lake covered perhaps twice the area it does at present. Sacred to Sobek the crocodile god (crocodiles were then plentiful in the district), its capital was Shedet on which stands the present city of Madinat al-Fayyum.

Dikes were built and villages established; Amenemhet III erected a large temple complex of which only the pedestals of two colossi remain; two other kings built

A fisherman brings his own shade to the brackish waters of Lake Qarun in the fertile Fayyum district south of Cairo. Since ancient times the lake, fed by the Nile, has shrunk considerably; but after recent stabilization of the water outflow, it is once more increasing in area.

A stonemason works on the restoration of the Temple of Hatshepsut in Western Thebes, which has been in progress for the last 20 years. Restoration of Egypt's monuments is a perpetual and continuous process, with a long history: the first recorded restorer was the Pharaoh Tuthmosis IV, who reigned from 1353 BC.

their pyramids at the southern entrance to the Fayyum itself. The mortuary temple of Amenemhet III at Hawarah, an extremely complex structure, probably gave rise to the Greek legend of the Labyrinth. East towards the Nile the Pyramid of Senusert II is notable for the pyramid town situated nearby, built to accommodate the workmen and later the practitioners of the cult of the king. It was discovered by Sir William Flinders Petrie (*d* 1944), one of the most remarkable of all Egyptologists and equal in status to Mariette (see p.14), though their methods were very different. He first visited Egypt in 1880 to survey the pyramids at Giza, and remained an indefatigable excavator there until 1920, excavating perhaps 40 sites. Unlike Mariette he was a systematic worker and published the results of all his excavations, often within months of completion. In addition to uncovering many new sites he introduced numerous new archaeological techniques.

SECOND INTERMEDIATE PERIOD (*c*1785-1550 BC)

Although the transition to the 13th Dynasty, seems to have been peaceful, a swift succession of briefly-reigning kings attests to their lack of status contrasted with that of the powerful chancellors. Serious trouble was to come from outisde Egypt's borders. Large-scale migrations of south-west Asian peoples into the Nile Delta inevitably led to conflict; invaders from the East known to the Egyptians as the Hyksos ('princes of the foreign lands') triumphed and founded the 15th Dynasty at Avaris, the city which they established in the Delta. The Egyptians managed to retain control of Thebes and King Kamose of the 17th Dynasty was able to gain the initiative and took his challenge to the walls of the Hyksos capital.

THE NEW KINGDOM (1540-1070 BC): THE EGYPTIAN EMPIRE

Kamose's brother Amose, first ruler of the 18th Dynasty, finally expelled the Hyksos from Egypt, pursuing them into Palestine and dispersing their allies. His successors built on his gains, making further conquests and alliances to raise Egypt to the status of an empire which reached its greatest extent, from central Sudan to the Euphrates, under Tuthmosis I (BC 1504-1492). A colony was established in Nubia under a viceroy and tributary yet autonomous states were permitted in western Asia, many of whose princes were raised in Egypt and returned to their own nations when adult. Hatshepsut, daughter of Tuthmosis I, became Egypt's most famous female ruler, later sharing her throne as joint 'king' with her stepson, Tuthmosis III. After her death he campaigned in Syria against the Mesopotamian Mitanni and established Napata as the capital of the Nubian colony. He attempted to erase all trace of his co-ruler's achievements by destroying her sculptured and painted images, but fortunately her spectacular mortuary temple remains, set beside that of Mentuhotpe on the west bank. Architectural patronage reached a new height under Amenhotpe III, when even the courtiers commissioned work of the highest quality to embellish their tombs, in the elegant style characteristic of the period.

The cultural efforts of the 18th Dynasty are most visible at Thebes (modern Luxor), the capital of New Kingdom Egypt. Here Amun, elevated to principal god and patron of the rulers, was venerated, and Thebes was transformed into a vast ceremonial city where successive rulers competed to build ever more magnificent temples. The escarpment on the west bank was chosen as the royal burial place, to be used by all the kings until the end of the 20th Dynasty. The temple of Karnak, north of Luxor, was added to by every pharaoh of the 18th and 19th dynasties. Mortuary temples were no longer attached directly to the tombs but were built as separate structures along the base of the hills facing the river. The present appearance of the monuments is the result of a century of diligent excavations by generations of archaeologists and the efforts of the Egyptian Antiquities Organization in restoring the buildings, but spectacular finds are still being made even in the most well-trodden areas.

By the 18th Dynasty Egyptian temples had achieved their classic form and little development subsequently took place. Great pylons – rectangular gateway towers, in the form of truncated pyramids – flanked the main entrance; they are usually identified with the goddesses Isis and Nephthys. At their bases were slots for banners, symbols of godhood. Inside, an open court led to the first chamber of the temple proper and then the great hypostyle hall – that is, with a pillar-supported roof - one or more smaller transverse chambers and then the sanctuary. Each hall was slightly elevated above its predecessor and each darker than the last. In the windowless sanctuary, a block of stone raised the naos, the shrine of the god, behind whose gilded doors the divine image was kept. Here the most sacred ceremonies were performed by the priests. Statues of gods, including the deified king, flanked the doors and aisles of the temple while the walls were painted or carved to illustrate the close relationship between the king and the gods. Surrounding the whole complex was a high perimeter wall to prevent observation by profane eyes.

The 50-year reign of Amenhotpe III was theologically orthodox with deference paid to Amun, but his son and successor Amenhotpe IV lost no time in promoting his own highly idiosyncratic vision. All other gods were rejected for the worship of the Aten, the disk of the sun. In furtherance of his ideal he changed his name to Akhenaten, abandoned Thebes and established a new city, Akhetaten in Middle Egypt opposite Hermopolis (Ashmunayn) exclusively for the adoration of the Aten. Palaces, temples of unique plan and whole streets of houses were quickly erected; tombs for himself and his officials were cut in the surrounding hills. His only associate in the complex

Ramesses II, whose 67-year reign began in 1304 BC, is probably the most ubiquitously represented of all the Pharaohs. In addition to his own enormous building programme, he restored the works of many of his predecessors, often replacing their images with his own. The example above is preserved in Cairo's Egyptian Museum.

rituals was his beautiful wife Nefertiti although sometimes their daughters appear in the reliefs and paintings. Not only was his religion unique – regarded by some scholars as the first known organized form of monotheism – but Egyptian artistic convention changed by royal command. Figures were elongated and subordinated to the person of the ruler and, of course, the sun-disk. The title 'pharaoh' (the word means 'great house', rather than 'king') was first used of the Akhenaten.

Akhenaten's successor, Tutankhamun, reinstated the worship of Amun. Akhetaten was abandoned to be dismantled by subsequent rulers so that little can now be seen standing at the site. During this period Egypt's Asian allies had been neglected; as a result, Egypt's control of the Middle East wavered and was challenged by the Hittites of Anatolia. Seti I, second king of the 19th Dynasty, revived Egyptian influence in Asia, holding the Hittites back in Syria; at home, he continued the embellishment of Thebes. Ramesses II gained renown as the greatest builder of ancient Egypt; as well as contributing to established sites like Thebes he built temples in many other sacred precincts, the most spectacular of which is the rock-cut temple at Abu Simbel. Not content with his own efforts, he usurped many of the monuments and statues of his predecessors and had his own name inserted on them. During his reign the capital was transferred from Memphis to a new city, Per-Ramesse, in the eastern Delta. From here he engaged in ineffective campaigns against the Hittites which were only concluded by a long-term treaty sealed by Ramesses' marriage to several Hittite princesses. The last of these campaigns, the Battle of Kadesh, is recorded in temple reliefs at Abydos, Luxor, Karnak and Abu Simbel.

The most serious threat to his successor was invasion by Libyans intent on settling. With Egypt disintegrating in a civil war, order was restored to the country by Sethnakhte, founder of the 20th Dynasty. Ramesses III, the most effective ruler of this dynasty, admired his predecessor Ramesses II to the extent of copying his buildings, for example his mortuary temple at Thebes, even to the battle scenes on the walls.

Reacting to the threat of invasion by a rebel viceroy of Nubia, Ramesses XI, last king of the 20th Dynasty divided regal authority with Herihor High Priest of Amun at Thebes.

THIRD INTERMEDIATE PERIOD (*c* 1069–525 BC)

This division remained the basis of rule in the following 21st Dynasty, with the high priests in the south often styling themselves kings. The Libyan immigrants, known as Meshwash or Ma, had been defeated and settled at various places in Egypt, yet they remained a cohesive group and gradually assumed enough power to seize the throne as the 22nd Dynasty. Nevertheless, from their capital in the Nile Delta, they continued the practice of appointing and sharing control with high priests.

Excavation is extremely difficult at Delta sites, as they have always suffered from the effects of the inundation and high water levels, while continued occupation has led to accumulated layers of modern building. Tanis, situated on natural gravel mounds, is one of the best-preserved sites, although nowhere near as impressive as those in the valley. It was probably saved by deterioration of the surrounding countryside after the incursion of Lake Manzalah, to the north, in the first centuries AD. Most of the great Egyptologists have investigated the site, which was built with the dismantled stones of Per-Ramesse, the great city of Ramesses II. But it remained for the French archaeologist Pierre Montet to reveal in 1939 the most important feature: the royal tombs of the 21st and 22nd dynasties in the precincts of the Temple of Amun. Some of them were undisturbed and while the treasure is impoverished compared to that of Tutankhamun, there were similarities in the funerary furniture and triple coffins, and especially in the sheet gold masks covering the heads of the deceased.

The Libyan hegemony disintegrated into several autonomous states and order was reimposed from an unexpected source. The colony established long before by the Egyptians at Napata in Nubia had been absorbed into the local population, though retaining much of its original culture and theology. Intensely devoted to Amun and apparently disturbed by the chaotic state of affairs in Egypt, the colonists' descendants invaded, and after defeating Tefnakhte of the 24th Dynasty their leader Shabaka established himself as king at Memphis.

Assyria was now a rising power to the east and a clash with Egypt was inevitable. The Assyrian king Ashurbanipal invaded several times between 667-3 BC, sacking Memphis and Thebes; while the last of the Nubian pharaohs retreated south to the safety of Napata. It was probably during this campaign that Ashurbanipal erected a fortress south of Memphis as a base for his assault against the city. Known as 'Babylon of Egypt', the Assyrian stronghold was to have great importance in later Egyptian history. Ashurbanipal left Egypt in the control of Delta princelings; after a period of confusion Psamtik I, with the assistance of Greek mercenaries, gained mastery and established the 26th Dynasty with his capital in the Delta city of Sais. During his reign of half a century the Greek presence in Egypt increased and under Amasis, the penultimate ruler of the dynasty and last of the great pharaohs, the Greeks were settled in their own enclave, the city of Naukratis. The Delta became the most important part of Egypt, with trade links throughout the Mediterranean.

LATE PERIOD (525-332 BC)

Persia succeeded Assyria as the greatest power in the East, quietly opposed by Amasis, who used some of Egypt's wealth to support Persia's enemies in south-western Asia. Annoyed by Egyptian policy and attracted by Egyptian wealth, the Persian ruler

Cambyses invaded and conquered the country in 525 BC, a year after the pharaoh died. Almost 3000 years of unbroken Egyptian rule came to an end.

Cambyses himself was remembered as a tyrant, but his successor Darius I honoured Egyptian ritual, completed a canal from the Delta to the Red Sea and built the Temple of Hibis at Khargah Oasis, still well-preserved and the only known monument remaining from the period 1110-300 BC.

Persian rule was relatively short-lived. Their defeat at Greek hands in 460 encouraged Egyptians to rebel, and independence was regained by Amyrteos, whose reign (404-399 BC) was the 28th Dynasty in its entirety. The Persians made repeated attempts to regain Egypt but Nekhtnebef I of the 30th Dynasty denied their ambition. Under him and his successors Egypt enjoyed the last flourish of native culture and prosperity. In 342 BC the Persians once more seized control of the country. Their dominion was destined to be brief: in 334, Alexander the Great of Macedon invaded Asia Minor from Greece.

THE MACEDONIAN AND PTOLEMAIC PERIODS (332-30 BC)

By 332, Alexander had destroyed Darius and seized his empire, including Egypt, where he was accepted as the legitimate king and installed at Memphis. After travelling to Siwah, where the oracle pronounced him the son of Amun, he halted on the north coast at the small village of Rhakotis, which he designated as the site of a new city. Thus was Alexandria founded, to prevail as the capital of Egypt for a thousand years. Leaving Egypt, Alexander engaged on his phenomenal Asian campaign but died in Babylon in 323. On his death, his empire was divided between his leading generals, of whom Alexander's successor in Egypt was Ptolemy Soter, who soon proclaimed himself King Ptolemy I.

Under Ptolemy and his successors, Greek administration replaced Egyptian bureaucracy; Egyptian architectural styles, however, were not ousted completely. In Alexandria and a few other cities buildings were erected in Greek style, but the rulers built many traditional Egyptian temples, in which they had themselves depicted in Egyptian dress with the ancient gods. In lesser buildings a strange amalgam of Egyptian and Greek artistic styles became common. Nearly all major sites throughout Egypt contain Ptolemaic contributions; at Denderah, Edfu and in the Fayyum Ptolemaic architecture replaced earlier buildings almost completely. So comprehensive and effective was the Ptolemaic administration that Greek became the country's official language, remaining so until the arrival of the Arabs.

While the first three Ptolemies proved to be exceptionally able and cultured rulers their descendants were no better than adventurers with a taste for murderous squabbles. Alliances between brothers, sisters, mothers and wives were made, broken and

re-made. One episode summarizes Ptolemaic politics. Ptolemy VIII Physkon ('fat-gut'), after murdering his nephew Ptolemy VII, married his own sister (his murdered nephew's widow) Cleopatra II, and then his niece,Cleopatra III. When Cleopatra II and their son Memphites declared themselves sole rulers Ptolemy VIII murdered Memphites. Soon after a reconciliation of the two Cleopatras, Ptolemy VIII died in 80 BC, bequeathing Egypt to another equally feckless generation.

Following the death of Ptolemy XII Auletes ('flute-player') in 51 BC, Egypt was left to his children. The most capable was Cleopatra VII, who married her brother Ptolemy XIII. Meanwhile, Egypt had begun to attract the interest of the ancient world's most terrifying power: Rome. Civil war held back Roman rapacity for a time but,

The colonnaded Temple of Isis, at Philae near Aswan, is one of the most intact of all Egypt's monuments. The temple was built relatively late, in the Greco-Roman era, but excavations have uncovered much earlier temples on the same site.

dragged Egypt into Roman politics. When the defeated Roman general Pompey sought refuge in Alexandria, Ptolemy XIII had him promptly executed. But Pompey's opponent, Julius Caesar, was far from being mollified. He declared war on Egypt.

During the ensuing conflict Ptolemy was drowned. Cleopatra speedily came to an accommodation with Caesar and after his recall to Rome (and assassination) was left with Caesar's child, Ptolemy Caesarian. Now Cleopatra chose the wrong side in Rome's continuing civil war. Having already married her second brother, Ptolemy XIV (whom she later had killed), she formed an alliance with Mark Antony. It was her dynasty's last error. Antony was defeated by Octavian, later Augustus Caesar, and both he and Cleopatra took their own lives in 30 BC. Octavian made Egypt into a Roman province, seizing all temple property as state assets and installing as governor a Roman prefect of equestrian rank.

Despite storms in high places, Alexandria under the Ptolemies had been queen of the Mediterranean, and she kept her standing under Imperial Rome. Great fleets left the Eastern Harbour for North Africa, the Levant and southern Europe while merchant ships from foreign ports filled the Western Harbour, all guided by the Pharos, an immense 100-metre lighthouse built by Ptolemy II and, like the pyramids, one of the wonders of the ancient world.

Laid in a grid pattern, streets lined with villas, gymnasia, baths, theatres and shops, led past the tomb of Alexander the Great to the Gate of the Sun at the west and Gate of the Moon at the east. Royal palaces built in Hellenistic style overlooked the Eastern Harbourand adjoining them were the Great Library and Museum, where directly under the ruler's patronage scientific and literary problems were unravelled by the greatest scholarsof the day. Euclid, benefiting from the experience of the ancient Egyptians, codified his theorems; Eratosthenes accurately measured the diameter of a round earth to within a few kilometres; while Sosegenes, again basing his work on that of the Egyptians, reformed the calendar for Julius Caesar. Other scientists developed wind, water and steam-driven engines merely to provide mechanical toys for the enjoyment of rulers. Also in Alexandria, a committee of Jewish scholars translated the Old Testament from Hebrew into Greek, increasingly the only language spoken by Egypt's Jewish community.

Alexandria was one of the main fountainheads of the new religion of Christianity; it was the seat of the principal bishop of Egypt, the Patriarch, who was the first to be styled pope. Alexandria also witnessed the first Christian persecutions under Septimius Severus at the end of the 2nd century AD and the horrendous assaults of Diocletian whohaving saved the city from famine – for which the so-called Pompey's Pillar was erected in his honour – turned the full might of his armies against the faithful.

THE ROMAN AND BYZANTINE PERIODS (30 BC – AD 640)

Few of the Roman emperors travelled to Egypt. The peripatetic Hadrian did so twice, and after his favourite Antinous drowned in the Nile founded the city of Antinopolis in his honour. Trajan, perceiving the tactical advantage of 'Babylon in Egypt', restored it and built a canal from it to connect with the ancient canal to the Red Sea. Much more sinister were the visit of Caracalla, who executed many young Alexandrians in response to an imagined slight, and Diocletian's energetic persecutions. But in general, as long as the revenues were returned and – most importantly – the grain exported, the emperors left the running of the country to their governors and contented themselves with having existing temples restored in their names or erecting triumphal arches.

The most important development was the introduction and growth of Christianity, which in Alexandria, despite the persecutions, had followed the general trend towards a hierarchy of bishops, priests and deacons. But in the rest of Egypt a new movement was emerging. About AD 270 St Anthony abandoned his patrician life and retreated into the desert, the first of many to pursue this form of solitary worship. His final retreat on the Red Sea is now a place of pilgrimage. West of the Delta at Kellia the desert is studded with the stone-built cells of these Desert Fathers who gathered together only for the Sabbath Eucharist and the great Christian festivals. A further development was made in Upper Egypt by St Pachomius, a former soldier who in 320 assembled a group of men under monastic rules of celibacy, communal prayer and work. Pachomius' ideas spread rapidly throughout Egypt, as attested by the ruins of hundreds of religious settlements from Aswan to Alexandria. Similar houses were formed for groups of women.

This simple carving of a Christian cross demonstrates the comparatively rustic quality of Coptic vernacular art compared to the sophistication of the earlier Greek or later Muslim styles.

These monasteries provided essential support for the Egyptian church in its theological contentions over the nature and substance of Christ, which ended in the severance of dialogue with the Catholic community after the Council of Chalcedon in 451. Called Monophysites by their opponents, Egyptian Christians have been known as Copts (from the Arabic version of the Greek word for Egypt) since the Islamic conquests; their significance declined but there are still active monastic communities in more isolated areas. One of the most thriving is that at Wadi Natrun, originally a collection of hermitages, founded about AD 330. Here four monasteries, each encircled by a high wall, contain several churches, the monks' residences and agricultural gardens.

Christians now form about ten per cent of the population and churches are still found in all the major towns. Some of the important cathedrals were enormous – that of St Menas in the Alexandrian Desert was patronized by three Christian emperors – and the remains of the Church of the Virgin at Ashmunayn are still impressive.

Near the Plain of Raha in the Sinai Peninsula, the Chapel of Aaron marks the traditional location where the wandering Israelites made the Golden Calf – and where Moses, on his return from Mount Sinai with the Ten Commandments, ordered its destruction.

THE MUSLIM PERIOD (from AD 640)

In the seventh century, the followers of the new religion of Islam erupted from their creed's birthplace in Arabia. Egypt fell by 642. A large town, Fustat, quickly grew up around the conquered Babylon fortress. It was first inhabited by the settled armies, and soon attracted others from the conquered territories. Arab tribes were settled in the Delta, over the years slowly making their way down the Nile valley. The Arabic language came to be used by native Egyptians, and many Copts converted to Islam. For two hundred years Egypt was a province of the Abbasid Caliphate of Baghdad under a series of governors but in 868 Ahmad Ibn Tulun, representative of the Abbasid Caliph in Baghdad, achieved independence. He built his own city near ancient Heliopolis but after his death the Caliphate re-asserted its power. Tulun's city was razed and only his great Mosque, built in the style of his native Baghdad, was left standing. It can still be seen today, a vast, arcaded mosque with an unusual minaret.

The architecture of mosques, which has changed little from the earliest days of Islam, is comparatively simple. Near the entrance stands the tall minaret from which the call to prayer is made. Inside, the axis of the mosque faces towards Mecca, which in Egypt is slightly south of east; the direction of prayer is indicated by a niche (*mihrab*). In front of this the *imam*, who can be any Muslim male of sound mind, leads the community in prayer. Beside is the *minbar*, a pulpit from which the sermon is read during the communal Friday prayer.

The thousands of mosques in Egypt and the number of churches are ample evidence of the seriousness with which the Egyptians consider their faith. Muslim worship can be solitary or communal, although the Friday prayer should be performed in assembly if possible. The statutory prayers consist of five short periods a day at specific times, when the call to prayer, nowadays usually enhanced by loudspeakers, rises up from the minaret of every mosque. While prayer is the most obvious display of faith the lives of Muslims are also ruled by the *shariah*, a set of religious laws which, although no longer the constitutional law, guide all aspects of behaviour.

The deep spiritual mood of worship is still evident, as is a joyful exuberance that almost certainly was apparent even in the early Muslim era. The combination of piety and delight is apparent both in public festivals and private ceremonies, where faith, affection and finery are at once displayed. Marriage, for example, consists of two ceremonies often months apart, the signing of the contract and the union of the couple, and both are conducted with boisterous display by the young male guests. Houses are covered with brilliant lamps and the bride and groom walk slowly to the venue for the function, surrounded by musicians, guests and often acrobats or clowns. The same delight informs every *mulid* – that is, a celebration, either national or local, to honour venerated men. The mulids of the Prophet Muhammad, Husayn or Sayyidah Zaynab are the most important in Cairo and can last several days with fairs, stalls selling sweetmeats and mementoes, entertainments for children, and the streets decorated with strings of coloured lights. Vast numbers visit from out of town and encamp around the mosque of the honoured deceased. Many important *mulids* are held in other cities – Qena, Dasuq or Luxor, for example. That of Sidi Badawi at Tanta attracts over a million visitors, while even in the fastness of the eastern desert hundreds of tents are pitched overnight for the mulid of al-Shadhili. The celebration during the month of the pilgrimage or at the end of Ramadan, besides necessitating communal prayers, are likewise opportunities for social gatherings. One particular secular festival, Sham al-Nasim, ('smelling the breeze'; the festival may well be have roots in ancient Egyptian practice) is a celebration of Spring when families and friends meet together to visit beauty spots and public gardens.

But if Egypt's Islamic practice has alway s been enthusiastic, the Islamic politics of earlier times were frequently stormy. Egyptian wealth was a magnet for power struggles. A semi-autonomous dynasty, the Ikhshids, was installed at Cairo in an

Decorations on a village house show that its occupant has made the Haj: *the pilgrimage to Mecca that is one of the most important duties in a Muslim's life. Returned pilgrims usually adorn their dwellings with scenes from their journey, always including the black-draped* Kabah, *the focus of Muslim devotions at Mecca.*

attempt to forestall the Fatimids, a people from western North Africa who claimed descent from Mohammed's daughter, Fatima. It was in vain and in 969 they fell to the Fatimid general Jawhar al-Sikilli. The very next day Jawhar laid the foundations of the city of Cairo (al-Qahirah, 'the victorious'), consisting of a walled enclosure which contained the palaces of his master al-Muizz, the Fatimid Caliph. His greatest work was the Mosque of al-Azhar, which continues to function today both as a mosque and as a university. Egypt thrived under its first Fatimid rulers, with the exception of al-Muizz's grandson, al-Hakim. He began his reign as a benign ruler, but degenerated into madness, murdering his subjects on whim, issuing laws designed to confine women to their homes, and venturing out only at night. Finally, one night in 1021, he rode into the Muqattam Hills and was never seen again.

Unlike all previous rulers the Fatimids were Shiah, a faction loyal to the Caliph Ali (*d* 661). His descendants believed that they had been unjustly deprived of the Caliphate; denied power, they had evolved an elaborate theology which contrasted with the simplicity of Sunni (traditional) Islam – a conflict within Islam that continues to this day. Shiism was never to attract any support from their subjects but the Fatimids did manage to reign for 200 years until the entry of the Crusaders into the Middle East. European aggression forced them to appeal for help from Syrian Muslim rulers, which allowed Salah al-Din (Saladin) to assume control in 1171 and found the Ayyubid house. The Ayyubids eventually controlled Syria and Palestine, but never ousted the Crusaders; in fact Egypt was attacked twice although both campaigns ended in disaster for the invaders.

The last effective Ayyubid ruler, al-Salih Ayyub, built up a large army of Turkish slaves (*mamluks*) imported from Crimea who soon aspired to power in their own right. When their chief, Aybak, married al-Salih Ayyub's widow, the throne was theirs. It was a bizarre system. Military slave origins were essential to promotion, even for the sultan, and perhaps because of their background the Mamelukes were notoriously given to murder and intrigue: there were more than 25 different rulers during the 132 years of Mamleuke domination. Yet it flourished against all odds, and Mameluke patronage produced some of the most beautiful Islamic monuments as well as artefacts in precious metals, glass, wood and fabric. Fort the most part the Mamelukes kept their deadly power struggles to themselves, leaving the native Egyptians, who provided essential administration and religious leaders, unmolested.

Caught up in the conflicts between the Ottomans and Persians, the Mameluke state finally fell in 1517 to the former who, ruling from Istanbul, reduced Egypt to a province once again. Later Ottoman governors were mere cyphers as the power was held by resurgent Mamelukes, the leaders of whom held the official title of Bey. Monuments in the Ottoman style outnumber all others in Cairo. Some of them are outstanding: the Sinan Mosque in Bulaq, the Mosque of Malikah Safiyyah and the Musafirkhanah Palace. The many hostelries, mosques, palaces and fountains indicate that Cairo was an extremely wealthy city.

Tiles on a Cairo wall show a typically Ottoman pattern, although with a certain provincial lack of finesse. Ottoman influence was widespread in Egypt, but it was rarely the result of direct imperial patronage, and the Ottoman models used by Egyptian craftsmen were not usually the finest.

FRENCH INVASION AND MODERN EGYPT (1798-)

British and French rivalry provoked a French invasion of Egypt in 1798 (the long-term objective was India), and although the expedition ended in failure it had several important results. It introduced European technology to Egypt and it broke the power of the Mameluke Bays, leaving a power vacuum. This last was filled by an ambitious Ottoman officer, Muhammad Ali, who by manipulating various factions established himself as governor and forced his former employers to grant his family hereditary rights of succession. Muhammad Ali was both ruthless and determined, and was not prepared to tolerate any threat to his power from a Mameluke resurgence. He removed the threat once and for all on the night of 1 March, 1811, when he invited the Mameluke leaders to a banquet. After the revels, his troops escorted the Mamelukes home along a narrow lane near the citadel; his troops sealed off both ends of the passage and all but one of the 470 guests were massacred. Muhammad Ali Pasha remained in power for 40 years, and oversaw a far-reaching building programme as well as the modernization of Egypt's institutions.

Another important result of the French invasion of Egypt was the discovery by French scholars and archaeologists of the country's heritage. The discovery of the Rosetta Stone in 1799 led to the deciphering of Egyptian hieroglyphic script by the historian Jean-Francois Champollion in 1818, and the foundation of modern Egyptology. In 1822, the publication of the *Description de l'Egypte*, the results of a French survey, brought Egypt's treasures to the attention of a wider audience.

Muhammad Ali's grandson Ismail gained the unique title Khedive – 'lord' – and a great deal of autonomy. During his reign, in 1869, the Suez Canal, linking the Red Sea to the Mediterranean, was opened. In 1875, however, Ismail was forced to sell his share in the canal to the British, and eventually to hand over the management of this finances to a French-British condominium. During the most active period of British expansionism Egypt was occupied in 1882; the country gained semi-independence 40 years later with the establishment of a kingdom under Ahmad Fuad in 1922; the British remained responsible for defence and, of course, the vital Canal.

British domination continued until after World War II. In 1952 King Faruq – whose failure to defeat the nascent State of Israel in the war of 1948-49 had made him increasingly unpopular - was deposed by the Organization of Free Officers, a group of young soldiers led by Colonel Gamal Abd al-Nasser, and Egypt was declared a republic.

Nasser's problems seemed insurmountable and his methods sometimes harsh but Egypt, now responsible for her own policies, progressed rapidly. One of Nasser's first acts – perhaps the most momentous in the history of Egypt – was to dismantle the great estates and distribute their holdings among the fallahin (farmers), who thus for the first time were in control of their own land. He also inititated efforts to expand and diversify the economy. Cotton, introduced to Egypt by Muhammad Ali and accounting for 80 per cent of exports, remains the main crop, but this is beginning to change. Egypt now produces most of its own consumer goods, and has laid the foundations for industrial development. Tourism and the revenues from the Suez Canal are major sources of income, although these can suffer badly from political events, as the Gulf War in 1991 demonstrated.

CAIRO: THE VICTORIOUS CITY

The legacy of this stupendous span of history takes concrete form in Cairo, a microcosm of Egypt. This immense capital has a daytime population of about 15 million – one quarter of Egypt's total – many of them workers who travel in from the Delta towns. With the constant traffic of cars, overloaded buses and donkey carts, the blaring of horns, the smog and the desert dust, Cairo's noise and dirt can be overwhelming. But so too are the wealth and variety of its treasures and ancient buildings.

Central Cairo is quite compact: it is only a short walk from the palatial colonial suburb of Garden City to the narrow medieval alleyways of the bazaar area, or from the Coptic centre of old Cairo to the flyovers and high-rise buildings of the business quarter.

The most venerable part of the city is Misr al-Qadimah to the south, the old city around the original fortress of Babylon. After the Arab conquest it remained the habitation of Christians and still contains several ancient churches and monasteries to which the Coptic Museum was added early this century. Unfortunately much of the Roman wall was destroyed in the 19th century but its distinctive pattern of stone and layered tiles can still be seen in places. Two cylindrical towers mark the old gatehouse; perched on top of one is the Monastery of St George, a Greek community and the venue of one of Egypt's most important Christian festivals. Inside the fort itself, some of the churches are extremely ancient; the church of St Barbara, dating from the 7th century, is especially well preserved. Al-Muallaqah, 'the hanging church' is so called because it is built on top of the Roman Gate, with its nave suspended above the passageway. Coptic Mass is still celebrated there every Friday and Sunday. One of the churches was sold to the Jews in Fatimid times and has served as the synagogue for the community in Egypt for centuries.

Just to the east of the fortress stands the Mosque of Amr which though now much enlarged, marks the location of the first mosque built in Africa immediately after the Arab conquest. Surrounding it are the ruins of the Arab city of Fustat, virtually destroyed by a Fatimid vizir in 1168 to prevent its falling to attacking Crusaders. Until then it had been a rival to Baghdad, a flourishing community with

Loose-robed pedestrians and a car shrouded against dust and sand are reminders that the European-style houses and pavement cafés of Cairo's business district belong firmly to the Middle East.

houses up to fourteen storeys high. Archaeologists have exposed foundations over large areas which display a sophisticated water distribution and sewage system and multi-roomed houses with wide tiled courtyards set with fountains and flower beds.

North on the river bank rises the great octagonal intake tower for the aqueduct that carried water to the Citadel; it was extended by successive sultans as accumulating silt caused the river to move westward. Here, at the entrance of the original canal which ran to the Delta and the Red Sea, the ancient ceremony of 'Cutting the Dyke' was celebrated, in late summer when the waters of the Nile were at an appropriate height and were let into the canal to feed the surrounding land. The canal, which ran though central Cairo, was filled in early this century and is now Port Said street, cutting north-east across the city. The height of the water was measured by the Nilometer on the southern tip of Roda Island opposite; its level helped predict the likelihood of a good harvest. The present Nilometer was built by an Arab governor, close to the site of an ancient predecessor, long since destroyed. The Nilometer's hereditary guardian and his descendants acted as heralds of the rise in water level until barrages were built in the last century.

Dominating the south-eastern corner of the city, Cairo's Citadel perches on the summit of an outcrop of the Muqattam Hills. Built by Salah al-Din (Saladin) during his refortification of the city, which he encircled with mighty walls, it was to remain the residence of the rulers and barracks of the principal corps of soldiers until the middle of the 19th century. It consists of two large enclosures set at intervals with towers. The residential southern enclosure originally contained the Striped Palace of the Sultan. It was demolished by Muhammad Ali to make room for his own great mosque which, although based on an Istanbul model, has come to symbolize Cairo. Muhammad Ali also built the Jewel Palace, now open to the public, which gives some idea of the extravagant life style of the former royal family.

Below the Citadel two imposing mosques, separated in time by 600 years, stand side by side. The older is that of Sultan Hasan (built 1356-62). Hasan was a young Mameluke ruler who in attempting to decrease the power of his emirs finally fell victim to their intrigues. His mosque is magnificent, and is still the largest in the city. Originally it was a *madrasah* (theological school), housing colleges for four schools of Islamic law. While much of the decoration has disappeared, some of it can still be seen in the main court and the chamber of Hasan's tomb. On the opposite side of the road is the Rifai Mosque, built in the 19th century for the mother of Khedive Ismail in flamboyant neo-Mameluke style.

The heart of medieval Cairo is the area further north surrounding the Mosque of al-Azhar. This was the centre of the great enclosure of al-Qahirah built by the commander Jawhar for the Fatimid Caliphs in 969, and remained a royal city, divorced from the commercial centre of Fustat, until opened to the populace by Salah al-Din in the middle of the 12th century. The palaces have been razed, replaced by later mosques, and the ancient walls were rebuilt in the 11th century but many of the roads retain their original alignment and names: al-Khiyyamiyyah ('tentmakers'), Suq al-Silah ('armourers'), Qafasin ('cagemakers') and so on. Only al-Azhar remains from the original city, the earliest Fatimid monument in Egypt. Here the first university was founded in the 10th century, continuing with its traditional syllabus for a thousand years until reformed in the early 20th century with extra faculties. Al-Azhar remains the most prestigious centre in the world for the study of traditional Islamic learning. Over 4000 students a year attend it free, studying all year round on mats in the courtyard of the mosque as well as in modern faculties.

Opposite al-Azhar stands the Mosque of Husayn, the principal mosque in Cairo and attended by the chiefs of state at the important festivals. The original mosque was a Fatimid foundation built in 1153 to house the head of al-Husayn, grandson of the Prophet Muhammad, who had died almost 500 years previously. The present building is 19th-century, although the original gateway still stands at one corner of the tomb. Running north from here is the ancient main thoroughfare, with some key Islamic monuments. The first section is known as al-Nahasin ('coppersmiths' quarter') where the principal merchandise is metalwork, both decorative and practical; further along, at al-Sagha, it is gold. On the northern side lies the bazaar area, a complex of narrow streets and alleyways known as the Khan al-Khalili. Built in 1382, it retains its medieval plan and function and is the centre for the manufacture and sale of decorative goods, in leather, wood, brass and more precious materials. Many of the workshops are open for inspection so that visitors can watch the craftsmen at work. Here bargaining is the rule, usually over mint tea. Nothing is sold for its stated price, and the more expensive the item, the more protracted the negotiation. It is quite in order to display outrage, shock or disappointment, provided it is done with *damm khafif* ('light blood', or humour). In the spice market, customers pause after sneezing to watch others who have entered do the same, as they have done since medieval times; although in those days they could not have refreshed themselves at Fishawi's cafe, once the meeting-place for literary expatriates, with a cup of the strong local coffee.

In this area, visitors can indulge in local foods in one of the many restaurants, though they may wish to avoid the specialists in brains, sweetbreads or cow's feet, and confine their experiments to kebabed lamb or rissoles, *mashwi* (stuffed vine leaves or aubergines), minced meat in crisp bread, pancakes with sweet or savoury fillings or, most traditional of all, *ful madames* (broad beans with olive oil and cumin), *tamiyyah* (bean rissoles) and *kushari* (pasta, chick peas and lentils covered with a fierce spicy chilli sauce). Sweets, usually taken in a special cafe, are innumerable: *zalabiya* (fritters dripping with rose syrup), *qatayf'* (shredded wheat with honey and nuts), *basbusah* (semolina cake) eaten with the delicious *ishda* (buffalo cream). As for the drinks,

A smith squats above his wares in one of Cairo's many thousand workshops. The domestic ironmongery he produces includes locks, which were in widespread use in Ancient Egypt almost 4000 years ago.

A Cairene attends to his prayers in the 14th-century Mosque of Barquq. Spacious and elegant, the mosque also demonstrates the austere simplicity required by Islam for religious buildings: nothing should distract the faithful from their devotions.

the choice is startling: fresh mango, *karkadayh* (brilliant red juice from the hibiscus), tamarind, carob, *zangabil* (ginger beer) and the juice of the sugar cane; some street vendors proffer a black liquorice-water that will strangle the unwary from inside.

The name of the main road beyond the Khan al-Khalili, Bayn al-Qasrayn ('Between the Two Palaces'), commemorates the great Fatimid palaces which once flanked either side. Four royal foundations are found here within 50 metres, between them encompassing 200 years of history. On the right the oldest is the Madrasah (college) and Tomb of al-Salih Ayyub, last Ayyubid sultan and on the left the tomb and mosque complexes of Qalawun, al-Nasir Muhammad ((1318) and Barquq (1386). Especially intriguing is the complex of the 13th-century sultan Qalawan, which besides the mosque contains his magnificent tomb, with some of the best mosaics in Cairo, and a hospital which was in continuous use from its building in the 1280s until the 1920s and even now is the site of an ophthalmic clinic. Bequests of the sultan also provided for the entertainment and feeding of the patients. Further north past Mameluke and Ottoman palaces, mosques, fountains and hostelries the road terminates at the fortress-like Mosque of al-Hakim, founded by al-Aziz in 990 and completed by his eccentric son, for whom it is named.

Surrounding Cairo are vast Muslim cemeteries, the large mausoleums of which,are built and furnished as if they were proper homes. Funerals are held within hours of death and are usually simple affairs, but there is a ceremony – *al-arbain* – held 40 days after the burials when large marquees are erected in public places where the Koran is read by professional reciters and chairs set out where guests visit the family and drink coffee. On the anniversary of a death, families will visit the tomb and eat a meal around the grave in memory of their loved one.

The tombs are visited by relatives only during these annual festivals of remembrance; for the rest of the year, they offer shelter to Cairo's homeless, whose numbers are now so great that the graveyards have virtually become towns in their own title. The practice is an old one: several of the sultans who built their tombs here also erected palaces, apartments and even markets, and made bequests for their upkeep.

The Southern Cemetery, or City of the Dead, contains the tombs of a number of much-venerated Muslims: Sidi Uqbah (*d* AD 677), a companion of the Prophet Muhammad; Dhul-Nun Misri, who introduced Sufism in the 9th century; and most highly honoured of all, the Imam Shafii (*d* 820) one of the original codifiers of Muslim law. This last Ayyubid tomb is particularly conspicuous, with its tall silvered dome crowned with a boat-shaped finial designed to hold seed and water for birds. Close by, Muhammad Ali Pasha built a mausoleum for his family where they repose in ornate, Turkish-style tombs.

Later Mameluke sultans built their tombs in the Eastern Cemetery where the most magnificent monuments include the mosques of Barquq (recently restored), Barsbay and Qayt-bay, the last perhaps the most beautiful of all Islamic buildings in Cairo. In the decoration of their great domes these three display the evolution of the stonemason's craft, one of the great strengths of Mameluke art, developing from the competent, continuous chevron of the Tomb of Barquq into the superbly balanced interplay of geometric fretwork and arabesques on the Tomb of Qayt-bay.

Several areas of Cairo have a distinct European ambience, the results of town planning by English or French designers. In Garden City on the Nile in central Cairo and in the suburb of al-Madi to the south, roads wind in rural English fashion among large mansions which would not be out of place in Surrey or Hampshire, although the cottage gardens are ablaze with frangipani, flamboyant, poinsettia and other semi-tropical vegetation. Heliopolis to the north of Cairo was the result of a single cohesive plan by Baron Empain, a Belgian. The Baron envisioned an enclave for Turks and Europeans, who would live in elegant palaces, with less lavish accommodation for administrative workers and peripheral apartments for the manual workers. The roads are laid in a formal radial pattern and the mansions and villas are built in neo-Mameluke style. For his own home, prominent now on the road from Cairo to the airport, Empain built an extravagant folly, with an exterior in the form of an Indian temple concealing a conventional Edwardian interior.

Behind the modern city and its medieval origins there is always the inscrutable majesty of Egypt's astonishing past. Historically, the pyramids of Giza and the Great Sphinx have nothing to do with the development of the city whose outskirts now lap towards their foundations; yet they are always deeply present, a bedrock of awesome permanence against which the bustling new apartment blocks and frenzied Cairene traffic seem as transitory as a scurrying ant-hill. This account of the city has no space to describe the great monuments, or the fabulous treasures in Cairo's Egyptian Museum. Still less can it convey the warmth and charisma of the Egyptians themselves, the city's greatest asset and a living link with an ancient culture that fascinates its modern inheritors at least as much as it does the many thousands of visitors who arrive from abroad each year.

This whole book, in fact, is only an introduction to Egypt: no single work this size could hope to be anything more. It is above all a visual introduction. The 'many marvellous things' that have astounded visitors for thousands of years have to be seen to be believed. David Couling's photographs, the fruit of many visits and much toil, convey better than any words both the majesty of Egypt's past and the vibrancy of its present. Arranged in a geographical sequence of essays, the pictures amount to a journey through space as well as time; and if they inspire readers to make the same journey for themselves, they will have served their purpose well.

◆

ONE

THE NILE

◆

Seen from a high-flying aircraft, most of Egypt is a flat expanse of dull brown and yellow sand. But from the Sudanese border in the south to the Mediterranean coast, the Nile stands out as a bright ribbon of living green. As they always have, more than 90 per cent of Egypt's people live almost within sight of the river, owing their very existence to the water and alluvial nutrients it carries to them from the heart of Africa.

The Nile and its seasonal inundations made the mighty pharaonic dynasties possible. The river not only fed them: it yielded enough surplus wealth to create the monuments that have awed visitors since the time they were built. Later, the Nile made Egypt the granary of the Roman Empire, and its delta is still the most productive area of North Africa.

For uncounted generations of Egyptians, the river was the great provider, the national transport system and the centre of social life. Fishermen sought the great Nile perch, cichlids and tiger fish in midstream, or netted catfish in the shallows; hunters stalked the fringing reeds – source of papyrus – for duck or other game, perhaps accompanied by the hunting cats so persistently depicted on tomb walls. Between the riverside cities, boats of all sizes plied the waters, from tiny fishing craft to freighters hauling quarried stone and the luxurious barges of the aristocracy.

Over the centuries, change has come slowly to the villages and towns along the banks. Dams and barrages control the inundations that once brought disaster as often

Near Luxor, the Nile flows sedately past a narrow strip of cultivated land against the backdrop of the Libyan Hills, so called because they lay in the general direction of Libya. Descending only 60 metres between Aswan and the sea, the river's progress is usually gentle, unless disturbed by contrary winds.

LEFT *A farmer hauls at a* shaduf *lifting frame to draw irrigation water from the Nile. The* shaduf *employs an array of levers and a mud counter-weight to raise a leather bucket; ancient wall-paintings show that it has been used for millennia, although its use is now restricted to small gardens.*

BELOW *His boat fully loaded, a reed-cutter returns with his harvest. Most of it will become animal fodder, although dried reeds are a useful source of basket material, while their stems are used to make crates. The papyrus stems that once served Ancient Egypt as paper are now very rare.*

as well-stocked granaries, and the placid silence of the river is often shattered by buzzing motorcycles and rumbling buses. But daily life continues much as it has always done: clothes and utensils are washed in the river, camels carry their burdens along elevated pathways, and farmers going about their business amble along the banks on donkeys. The houses themselves are more likely to be made of concrete than the mud bricks of old, but they are built and decorated with picturesque conservatism to patterns that are often as ancient as the Nile's first civilizations.

◆

His boat safely moored in the shallows, a Nile fisherman mends his nets. The river provides a huge yield of fish, all edible, from the sluggish catfish to the giant and highly active Nile perch that was venerated in ancient times.

LEFT *Blue water hyacinths fill a Nile-side pool. The plants (*Eichhornia*) were introduced from South America for their decorative charm; however, they thrive to excess in Egyptian conditions, and are now considered a pernicious weed: great efforts are needed to keep even a wide watercourse unchoked.*

Framed by a luxuriant palm grove, a riverside village appears deceptively tranquil. Nile farmers are usually in constant activity, maintaining canals, drains and irrigation dikes as well as ploughing, sowing and harvesting. The strip of land beside the river yields almost all of Egypt's agricultural produce, from corn to sugar-cane and dates.

Reeds line the river as it passes close to the Theban Hills near Luxor. In ancient times, Nile reeds were far more extensive: the wild-fowler in his boat, hunting his prey through endless banks of them, is a recurring theme in tomb paintings.

St Catherine's Monastery nestles close to the foot of Mount Sinai, according to tradition the site where Moses encountered the Burning Bush. The Roman Emperor Justinian built a church here in 526, providing it with monks and guards to protect them. The monastery has ever since remained under the authority of the Greek Orthodox Church.

In a typical Sinai landscape, gravel plains are interrupted by the coloured rock of starkly rising mountains. Arid and seemingly inhospitable, Sinai supports a surprising range of animal life, including wolves and, until the 1940s, leopards.

The domed tomb of Nabi Salih stands on a rocky crest in southern Sinai near St Catherine's monastery. The prophet is mentioned several times in the Koran, which tells how he admonished his people. Nabi Salih's tomb is the scene of an annual religious festival.

A channel cut into a Sinai hillside serves to direct some of the peninsula's sparse rainfall into a deep cistern. Such rain channels are mostly the work of Sinai's Bedouin nomads, who usually enlarge existing natural cracks in the rock.

LEFT *Two Bedouin girls display their festival clothes, quite unlike the costumes worn by women in the rest of Egypt. Muslims noted for their devoutness, the Sinai Bedouin live according to their own strict and complex traditions; when these girls marry, for example, they will transfer to the camp of their husbands.*

ABOVE *Goats graze on the scanty vegetation around a Bedouin encampment. The Bedouin are scattered throughout Sinai, although their numbers are shrinking; they are usually less nomadic than their kinsfolk elsewhere in the Middle East, but they still live in tents and are always prepared to move to better pastures if necessary.*

RIGHT *A pomegranate bush bursts into spring flower at the edge of an orange grove. Areas favoured by local micro-climates are often tended by Bedouin as surprisingly productive orchards.*

BELOW *Heavily veiled as the Bedouin code requires, an old woman reveals only her eyes and her hands, gnarled by a lifetime of toil in a harsh environment.*

At a temporary encampment in Sinai, a Bedouin tent provides the only protection for an entire family. The tents, woven from goat hair, are light, durable and easily packed on camels when it is time to move on.

Scorched date palms lend an air of devastation to a Sinai orchard. In fact, so long as the trees' delicate crowns are spared fire actually increases the yield of the palms; they are regularly burned by their Bedouin cultivators.

ABOVE *Heading from the Mediterranean to the Red Sea, ships steam slowly through the Suez Canal. Recently widened to accommodate all but the largest supertankers, the Canal remains a vital artery of world commerce – and a major source of Egyptian revenue.*

RIGHT *A burnt-out Israeli tank bears witness to the savage battles of 1973, when an Egyptian attack across the Suez Canal surprised Israel and recaptured some of the Sinai peninsula, territory lost six years before.*

FOUR

CAIRO: HEART OF EGYPT

◆

The largest city in Africa – and the Middle East – Cairo's origins go back to AD 641, when Egypt's Muslim invaders established their capital of Fustat around the old Fortress of Babylon. Successive dynasties built their own palace-cities to the north of the 7th-century foundation, culminating in 969 when the Fatimids founded al-Qahirah and gave the modern city its name. Saladin in the 12th century fortified the rebuilt city with a massive wall and a protecting Citadel. Over the next four centuries, Cairo grew into one of the world's richest commercial centres, outshining even Baghdad and boasting a population of 500,000. Later, under Ottoman rule, its importance diminished; it did not regain its medieval population until the late 19th century.

From then on, though, its growth was explosive: one million in 1927 became two million 20 years later, eight million by 1976 and at least 15 million today. Teeming with life and colour, Cairo and its traffic can overwhelm even its own citizens and regularly exhausts visitors, drawn as much by the rural vitality of its street life and bazaars as by its unique assembly of historic monuments.

Seen from Cairo's Hilton Hotel, Gezira Island looks like the opposite bank of the Nile. The island includes the grounds and racecourse (left) of the Gezira club, once the exclusive retreat of the foreign community. It is now open to all comers, although high admission charges still keep most ordinary Cairenes out.

The Cairo conurbation may soon include the most famous monument in the world. Giża on the Nile's west bank, still technically the capital of a separate province, has already been absorbed by its expanding neighbour. The spreading tide of urbanization is now lapping around Giza's most celebrated attractions: the Pyramids and the great Sphinx.

The Giza pyramids mark the northern extremity of the necropolis of the ancient city of Memphis. But the rest of that astonishing cemetery has nothing quite able to match Giza's Great Pyramid of Khufu, one of the most ambitious single projects ever successfully completed by the human race. Although the fine limestone that once encased it has long since been torn away to build much of Cairo, reducing its height from 145 to 135 metres, its perfection still staggers the imagination. Aligned precisely with the cardinal points of the compass – a device unknown to its architects 4500 years ago – it is the only one of the seven wonders of the ancient world that still survives.

◆

LEFT *The 9th-century Mosque of Ibn Tulun (dome, centre) is almost overwhelmed by the expanding modern city. To the right, a double dome marks the Mosque of Sarghatmish; the high-rise towers of the Qasr al-Nil business district dominate the skyline.*

BELOW *A young Cairene and her father stroll past the Edwardian frontage of Groppi's Café. Famously patronized between the wars by Cairo's fashionable rich, Groppi's is still renowned for its ice cream.*

ABOVE *Southernmost of the gates of the old Fatimid city of al-Qahirah, the Bab Zuwaylah was named after a regiment recruited from Berbers, whom the Shiite Fatimids were more prepared to trust than the region's more numerous Sunni Arabs. In the 15th century, the Sultan Muayyad Shaykh used the gate towers as bases for the twin minarets of his adjacent mosque.*

RIGHT *A shop in the district of al-Ghawriyyah is the last still to make the felt* tarboosh, *using brass moulds to shape each hat to a customer's head. Originally worn beneath a turban, in the 19th century the tasselled* tarboosh *became the archetypal Egyptian head-gear. Today, it is mostly worn only by leaders of religious institutions.*

LEFT *Cairenes enjoy a sociable smoke from a café's* sisha, *the traditional Egyptian water pipe. Tobacco smoke is cooled by its passage through long tubes and the water-bowl; one pipe is usually shared by several companions. In this case, all are wearing the* galabiyyah, *a robe common in Egypt since at least Ptolemaic times.*

RIGHT *A duck seller displays his stock in a Cairo street. Most Egyptians prefer to buy their poultry live; these birds are restrained by a cage made from split palm stems.*

LEFT *Workers load trucks outside a Cairo brickworks. The Nile banks around the city were once lined with brick factories, which used the rich black riverside soil to bake bricks that fired to an attractive pale red. So much agriculturally valuable soil was consumed that most have now been forced to close.*

Flanked by minarets, the domed tomb chamber of the Mosque of Sultan Hasan contains the remains of its 14th-century founder. The Mosque is the largest madrasah – *theological college – in Cairo.*

The magnificent portal of Sultan Hasan's mosque is set at an angle to the main building, an unusual arrangement brought about by the Sultan's wish for a fine view of his proudest achievement from his palace in the nearby Citadel.

The Mosque of Muhammad Ali Pasha, completed in 1848, was based entirely on an Istanbul model and owes nothing to native Egyptian styles. Inside is a clock given by the King of France in exchange for an ancient obelisk from Luxor (page 109). The clock has never worked, but the obelisk still stands in Paris.

Shaded and cool, pillared arcades surround the exterior of Muhammad Ali's mosque. The arcade walls, lined with alabaster in the Turkish style, were once translucent; in recent years, they have become badly discoloured by the dust and pollution of modern Cairo.

A tree-lined avenue in the Eastern Cemetery leads to the tomb of the Khedive Tewfiq, during whose reign the British occupied Egypt in 1882. Their object was to seize control of Egyptian finances; but enough was spared to provide the Khedive with a mausoleum in fine, neo-Mameluke style.

Capped by a limestone dome carved in a fretwork of interlocking stars and arabesques, the exquisite 15th-century Mosque of Sultan Qayt-Bay in the Northern Cemetery contains the tomb of the Sultan, an extravagant spender with a contrasting reputation for acts of casual violence.

LEFT *Elaborately corbelled and painted, the lantern ceiling beneath the dome of the Qayt-Bay mosque is the main source of interior light. Before the mid-14th century, roofs were almost unknown in Cairo's mosques; most were open enclosures.*

RIGHT *Stained-glass windows glow dimly in the cool interior of the Mosque of Qayt-Bay. Unlike their Western counterparts, Islamic craftsmen usually created geometrical or foliate motifs, set in stucco frames: their religion discouraged them from representing human figures*

Serene beneath its chevron-patterned dome, the Mosque of Barquq is also the burial place of the 14th-century Sultan, who had it built in Cairo's Eastern Cemetery close to the tombs of the most pious Muslims.

ABOVE *Stone pillars support high arches in the Mosque of Barquq. To the right of the* mihrab *(prayer niche) stands the* minbar*, the pulpit from which the Friday sermon is preached.*

RIGHT *The doors of Sultan Barquq's mosque are a fine example of* mashabiyyah*, the Egyptian art of creating decorative windows, screens and doors from turned wooden pieces fitted together, jigsaw-like, without the use of glue.*

BELOW *A carved stele between the paws of the Great Sphinx commemorates the monument's restoration by Tuthmosis IV in the 14th-century* BC. *The inscrutable, 50-metre Sphinx, carved from a natural rock outcrop, is of uncertain antiquity; it has been baffling its visitors for more than four millennia.*

ABOVE *Seen in close-up, exposed building blocks obscure the perfect shape of the Great Pyramid of Khufu. Even without the polished façade that once covered the block, the pyramid stands almost 150 metres high. With a base area of more than four hectares, it accounts for about 2.3 million cubic metres of stone.*

LEFT *The greatest of Egypt's pyramids loom over a dusty Giza skyline. A slight elevation makes Khafre's pyramid seem the largest, but the Great Pyramid itself is on the right, built about 2600* BC *by Khafre's father Khufu. The smaller pyramid of Menkaure, less than half as massive, completes the ancient triad.*

FAYYUM

Centred around the salt lake of Qarun, 100 kilometres south-west of Cairo, Egypt's Fayyum province is a deep green bowl amid the desert. The lake is over 40 metres below sea level; the descent of its feedwater from the Nile has laced the Fayyum with a pattern of fast-moving streams quite different from the stately progress of the great river itself.

The region's development into one of the country's most productive areas began around 1850 BC, when Amenemhet III began to regulate the flow of Nile water into the lake. It became a resort area for Egypt's rulers, and, later, the Crocodilopolis of the Greeks, who were fascinated by the abundant reptiles. Medieval neglect and misgovernment caused a deep decline that was not reversed until modern times, but Fayyum, with a population now standing at more than three million, is once more the country's largest oasis, and a popular resort with Cairenes, who go there to bathe in the mineral springs at Ayn Sillin.

◆

ABOVE *Women wash clothes in a Fayyum backwater, a daily event that combines cleanliness with sociability. In former times, it could be a hazardous business: the area had Egypt's highest crocodile population.*

LEFT *Near the town of Biyahmu, two 10-metre pedestals are all that remain of gigantic statues of the 19th-century* BC *King Amenemhet III. He was responsible for major water-control and land reclamation work in the Fayyum; the statues may well once have fronted a celebratory temple.*

Built during the Claudian years of the Roman Empire, the Temple of Karanis in the Fayyum was dedicated to Pnepheros and Petesuchos, two of many Greco-Roman names for the crocodile god Sobek. The temple's own crocodiles were kept in a sacred pool; after death, they were mummified and buried in nearby cemeteries.

Bahr Yusuf, 'River of Joseph', nears its outlet in Lake Qarun. The river waters the whole of the Fayyum, entering the district at Lahun, where rulers since Amenhemhet III have controlled its flow with sluices and other regulators.

Driven solely by the force of descending water, one of the so-called 'roaring' water-wheels of the Fayyum transports mainstream water into an irrigation ditch. Elsewhere in the Nile valley, the sluggish water flow means that such wheels have to be powered by men, animals or motors.

LEFT *The ornate towers of a pigeon house stand above a heavily irrigated Fayyum meadow. Pigeon, fed on the local grains and pulses but allowed for the most part to roam freely, is one of the great delicacies of the country.*

BELOW *Restrained by his owner's rope, a camel surveys the lush greenery of the Fayyum. Superbly adapted to life in the desert, camels are also essential beasts of burden in well-watered villages throughout Egypt.*

FIVE

THE RIVER ROAD TO THEBES

Denderah, Abydos, Ashmunayn

◆

The 450-kilometre stretch of the Nile between Memphis and Thebes – modern Luxor – was probably the most travelled section of the river in ancient times, just as it is today. On the western bank the pyramids of the great necropolis of Memphis pass before the traveller in stately review: Saqqarah, Dahshur and Maydum, where the distinctive Bent Pyramid of Sneferu stands, second in volume only to the Pyramid of Khufu at Giza. It is 125 kilometres before the first major town, Beni Suef, at the edge of the well-watered Fayyum district; close by is the site of Herakleopolis. Around 2250 BC, as Ninsu, it was briefly the dynastic capital of Egypt; upstream from the ruined city, the central region usually known as Middle Egypt begins.

Doubly nourished by the slow-moving Nile itself and the fast-running Bahr Yusuf – 'Joseph's River' – to the west, the left bank is intensely cultivated for more than 100 kilometres, to the city of Al-Minyu and beyond to Mallawi on the east bank. Just north of Mallawi,at Ashmunayn, lies the waterlogged site of Hermopolis, city of the moon-god Thoth and once the capital of the ancient Egyptian *nome* – administrative district – to which it gave its name. Dating from the reign of Nekhtnebef I, the main temple is much ruined; nearby are the remains of a Ramesside temple of Amun, while south of the temple area stand the pillars of a 5th-century basilica, whose columns in turn were once part

The heavily restored temple of Seti I , with its formal square columns, is the best preserved of Abydos' many monuments. It was begun by Seti but only completed in the reign of his son, Ramesses II; the later work is clearly of lower quality.

of an earlier Hellenistic temple built by Ptolemy III Euregetes in the 4th century BC.

The necropolis of the city lies to the south-east at Tunah al-Gabal where galleries contain mummified baboons and ibis, creatures sacred to Thoth; across the river two cemeteries contain rock-cut tombs of the governors of Hermopolis.

Farther south along the eastern bank, King Akhenaten erected his new capital of Akhetaten in the 14th century BC. The city was dedicated to Aten, 'father and mother of all creation', in whose zealous service the king erased many mentions of older gods and greatly distressed a conservative priesthood. But despite its vast size and careful planning, Akhetaten barely outlived its unpopular creator: later kings dismantled it almost completely. Much of its masonry became part of Hermopolis; besides the tombs in the hills behind the city, only the foundations of Akhetaten's many palaces and temples now remain.

About 100 kilometres farther upstream, the holy city of Abydos marks the edge of Middle Egypt's cultivated land. It was a cult centre of great significance to ancient Egyptians and a place of pilgrimage, if not in life then in death, for all made provision for the journey here to meet Osiris, Judge of the Dead, in the Afterworld. Abydos was the southern necropolis of Egypt's early rulers, who had tombs or cenotaphs built here; in time, one of them was assumed to belong to Osiris himself. The best-preserved temple is that of Seti I, dating from the 13th century BC. It is distinguished by its L-shaped form and its several courts, the square pillars that raise its portico, and its dedication to no less than seven deities, including the divine King Seti himself. Inside are some of the most impressive reliefs of the period, some of them retaining their original brilliant colours. Clumsy work in the hypostyle hall – the term describes a roof supported by pillars – completed by Seti's son, Ramesses II, contrasts with the fine craftsmanship shown in the seven chapels of the gods: Horus, Isis, Osiris, Amun, Re, Ptah and Seti. Tableaux show the rituals performed by the king for the gods but in his own chapel, they emphasize his omnipotence.

BELOW *An immense stone baboon, one of a pair carved in the 14th century BC, still stands guard over a Temple of Thoth at Hermopolis. Unfortunately, the moon-god's temple has long since crumbled: only the baboons remain, perhaps saved from destruction by their bulk.*

RIGHT *A set of columns with fine, classical capitals are all that remains of the Church of the Virgin at Ashmunayn, once an important Christian centre. It was built about AD 430 using blocks taken from a temple of Ptolemy II; in time, the church too was plundered for its valuable building materials.*

LEFT *A mud-brick pigeon-house, plastered and painted to resemble a fortress, stands amid palm trees at Ashmunayn. Such houses, where birds are bred for the table, are a distinctive feature of the Egyptian countryside, and are often extremely elaborate.*

There is also a king list, naming many Seti's predecessors to predynastic times; its many omissions include the hated Akhenaten.

Upstream, the river follows a wide curve to the west before turning south at Denderah (Tentyra). There, on the west bank, lies the precinct of the cow-goddess Hathor, her consort Horus of Edfu and their child Ihy. The whole complex is remarkably well-preserved; its enclosed courtyard is now filled with statues found at other areas of the site. Much of the structure is Ptolemaic but the main hypostyle hall is Roman; on its supporting pillars are sculpted heads of Hathor, defaced in Christian times.on religious grounds.

The temple's roof shrines, though, have escaped the attention of pious vandals. One rooftop pavilion was used in the ceremony of 'Union with the Sun', when sacred images were ritually revived by exposure to sunlight. Two other pavilions were for the cult of Osiris. The Denderah temple was primarily a healing centre, as indicated by a supplication image of Horus; amid the sacred architecture, its practically-minded builders included a sanatorium for convalescents.

◆

LEFT *Inside the Temple of Ramesses II at Abydos, a painted relief advertises the merits of various towns and districts of Egypt. A personification of each offers the choicest products of his region, including bread and fruit on the right, and wine on the left.*

LEFT *In a surviving temple of Thoth at Hermopolis, a relief shows Ramesses II peering over Thoth's shoulder as the ibis-headed god writes the king's name. The persistence of the written word, at least when inscribed in stone, was strongly associated with immortality.*

RIGHT *Hieroglyphs describing life in the 13th-century* BC *reign of Seti I decorate the columns of the king's temple. Ostensibly dedicated to Osiris, the temple also celebrated the authority of the king himself.*

The Theban Hills, seen here across a field of cut wheat at the limits of cultivable land, marked the beginning of the kingdom of death. For the Egyptians, the realm of the dead was always to the west, associated with the setting sun that slid behind the escarpment and began its night journey through the underworld.

Seen from the surrounding cliffs, the terraces of the Mortuary Temple of Hatshepsut ascend in elegant succession to the rock-cut shrine itself. Although styled a 'king' in most inscriptions, Hatshepsut was the most powerful woman to reign in her own right in ancient Egypt, from 1503 to 1482 BC.

ABOVE *In the Chapel of Hathor in Hatshepsut's temple, pillars bear as their capitals the carved image of the goddess, 'The Mistress of the West'. Since Hatshepsut's temple was in the western hills, it was considered Hathor's home.*

The severe lines of the façade of Hatshepsut's Mortuary Temple at Deir al-Bahri are interrupted by statues of the queen herself standing before the pillars; originally, the outline was further softened by groves of shrubs that were planted throughout the temple courtyards.

LEFT *The Ramesseum, mortuary temple of Ramesses II, stands alone in a waste of sun-scorched rock. When it was built, in the 13th century* BC, *the complex included not only the main temple but also a brick-built palace and a vast warren of storerooms for the upkeep of the priesthood and their ceremonies.*

RIGHT *A gateway to the Mortuary Temple of Ramesses III imitates the form of a Syrian fortress. The purpose was to emphasize Egyptian control of Syria, although it was more wishful thinking than historical record: by Ramesses' death in 1166* BC, *Egypt's influence in the region had vastly diminished.*

Headless and mutilated, the remains of enormous statues of Ramesses II stand outside his mortuary temple. One head inspired Shelley's poem, 'Ozymandias' – the Latin version of the great king's name.

Scarred from the erosion of more than 2000 years, the Colossi of Memnon have attracted visitors since Greco-Roman times. The misnamed statues were thought by the Greeks to be representations of the Trojan hero Memnon; in fact, they are all that remains of the Mortuary Temple of Amenhotpe III.

SEVEN

LUXOR AND KARNAK

◆

Al-Uqsur, it is called in Arabic: 'the Palaces'. Yet for more than a thousand years, Luxor's palaces were not even a memory. The little agricultural village, on the Nile bank far upstream from Egypt's population centres – Cairo is almost 700 kilometres away – was renowned not for its architecture but for the annual festival with which it celebrated the eminent 13th-century Sufi Shaykh Yusuf Abu al-Hajjaj.

In the early 19th century, though, French archaeologists discovered that the sleepy village deserved its name. Beneath the mosque that was built around Shaykh Yusuf's tomb, a vast temple lay buried; more ruins were hidden nearby. Below Luxor and adjacent Karnak lay none other than the southern pharaonic capital of Thebes, a city already flourishing in the third millennium BC. As Waset, the cult centre of Amun, omnipotent chief of all the gods, it reached its zenith between 1540 and 1350 BC, during the Egyptian Empire of the 18th and 19th Dynasties. Of all Egyptian cities, only Memphis could match it in size or wealth; and

The Temple of Luxor was built around 1350 BC by Amenhotpe III in the high days of Egyptian imperial power. Until the late 19th century, its majestic colonnades were buried beneath Luxor's streets and houses; a mosque, constructed on one of the temple's great pylons, is still in use.

whereas Memphis in decline was pillaged of its masonry to build nearby successor cities, Thebes was largely preserved by its isolation.

Although its mud-brick palaces and houses have crumbled before the eroding forces of wind and sand, the stone-built temples and monuments survive intact enough to stagger the imagination, especially the vast Temple of Amun at Karnak, where avenues of sphinxes lead to an imposing complex of courts and pylons, obelisks and colossi, and halls decorated with paintings and reliefs.

◆

ABOVE *Multi-decked modern tourist cruisers and traditional Nile feluccas pass the quays of Luxor. The town, for centuries a forgotten backwater, only began to resume importance in the mid-19th century, with the renewed interest in the ruins of the ancient city of Thebes.*

Two great stone pylons outside the Temple of Luxor, arranged in the shape of the hieroglyph for hills, afford the temple symbolic shelter. The pylons were once accompanied by two 25-metre obelisks, but only one now remains on the site: its companion was presented to France in the 19th century, and now stands in the Place de la Concorde in Paris.

An avenue of sphinxes leads from the Temple of Luxor to the nearby temple complex of Karnak, just to the north. The sacred images of Karnak's deities – Amun, his consort Mut and their son Khonsu – were carried to Luxor during the temples' principal festivals.

Despite the Roman origins of its patrons, the pillared hall of the Temple of Esna, south of Luxor, preserves the form and decoration of older Egyptian traditions. It was dedicated to the gods Khnum and Khonsu, respectively the god of the Nile cataracts and the moon god; the columns are inscribed with important texts for religious festivals and ceremonies.

RIGHT *Broken statues lie scattered across the colonnade of the Temple of Horus at Edfu. In the temple's heyday, such statues were rarely destroyed, even when they were due for replacement: as objects of power and holiness, they were usually given a ceremonial burial inside the sacred precincts.*

BELOW *Guarding the temple forecourt at Edfu, a fearsome stone falcon displays some of the sterner characteristics of the god it represented: Horus, the epitome of divine kingship.*

RIGHT *Reliefs in the Temple of Horus show scars from the temple's occupation by early Christians. Many Egyptian monuments have suffered from such righteous defilement, with carved and painted images defaced and covered over with plaster.*

LEFT *The double entrance to the Temple of Sobek and Horus at Kom Ombo opens into twin corridors that lead to the respective sanctuaries of the two gods; the shrine of Sobek, the crocodile god, is on the right. Each had his own priesthood and ritual; celebrations were combined at their great joint festivals, held at the height of the Nile inundation when crocodiles were rife.*

A pillared corridor leads to the shrine of Sobek deep in the heart of his Kom Ombo temple. Sunlight flooding through the vanished roof now dispels the mystery of the crocodile god's sanctuary; once, the only illumination came from the dim lamps of the priesthood.

In a graphic demonstration of his strength and power, the figure of a ruler looms from a column in the Kom Ombo temple complex. He holds an ankh *in his hand, the symbol of life; it was later adapted by Coptic Christians as the* crux ansata, *their version of the crucifix.*

Depicted on the walls of his sanctuary at Kom Ombo, the crocodile god Sobek is seated on a pedestal that takes the form of the hieroglyph for a water channel. Like many other deities, Sobek had a solar aspect, here demonstrated by the sun disk above his head.

ABOVE *Horus of Ombos, in his usual form of a hawk-headed man, gives a curved dagger to King Ptolemy VIII in a Kom Ombo relief. The king wears the* hemhemet, *an elaborate horned crown made from papyrus; the women accompanying him are Cleopatra II and Cleopatra III, respectively his sister and his niece but both of them his wives.*

RIGHT *In another Kom Ombo carving, Ptolemy VIII wears a double crown for the* heb sed *jubilee, an ancient ceremony that celebrated any king who had reigned for 30 years.*

NINE

ASWAN AND BEYOND

◆

Aswan, 240 kilometres north of the modern frontier with Sudan, marks the beginning of what was formerly Lower Nubia, once a near-trackless desert and now submerged by Lake Nasser since the completion of the Aswan High Dam, built in the 1960s to control the Nile's seasonal inundations. Although Egyptian authority often extended much farther south, pharaonic power was always disputed, and in ancient times Aswan was reckoned the last truly Egyptian city. It controlled the valuable trade in gold, ivory, incense, exotic animals and slaves, and its viceroys were powerful figures. They have left their tombs in rock-cut chapels high on the cliffs of the west bank, marked today by the medieval Dome of the Winds. Ancient Aswan itself was built on Elephantine Island, highly defensible against Nubian attack, and the site of the glorious temple of ram-headed Khnum, the patron god of the city.

Aswan remained an important frontier town under later Christians and Muslims both; the Monastery of St Simeon and a large 11th-century Muslim cemetery are the most obvious reminders of their presence. The modern city has one of the most pleasant aspects in Egypt and was considered the perfect place for convalescence. For most visitors today, Aswan is the gateway to the awesome temples of Abu Simbel, 240 kilometres to the south, probably the most striking remains from Egypt's New Kingdom.

Four 20-metre statues of Ramesses II guard the entrance to the Temple of Abu Simbel, each stone eyelid large enough for a child's bed. The 13th-century BC temple, almost totally buried in sand, was rediscovered in 1813; the task of uncovering its megalomaniac images took twenty years.

The temples were built by Ramesses II as part of a programme intended to display the full might of Egypt and her king to the potentially rebellious Nubians. More than 3000 years later, the High Dam building programme threatened to destroy Ramesses' creation. The great dam was capable of trapping more than 150 billion cubic metres of water in the new lake Nasser, which would cover most of the Abu Simbel site. In an international operation which took five years and cost $9 million, the Temple of Hathor and the Great Temple, both built into the rock, were cut out of their original cliff site and moved to higher ground.

Downstream from Aswan stands Philae, the so-called 'Pearl of the Nile', a group of temples dedicated to Isis and Osiris. They are considerably less ancient than the buildings at Abu Simbel: begun under the Ptolemaic monarchy in the fourth century BC, the temples were the last refuge of the old religion until Justinian finally closed them in the 6th century AD. Philae, too, narrowly escaped drowning. Already damaged by rising water levels caused by earlier dam-building, like Abu Simbel it was moved piece by piece in the 1960s to its present island.

◆

Elephantine is by far the biggest of the islands scattered across the Nile at Aswan. The longest-inhabited part of the city, the island was a powerful frontier fortress; its name, a Greek translation of the Egyptian 'Abu', 'land of the elephant', probably derives from the large, grey boulders in the surrounding river, rather than real elephants.

The 20th-century tomb of Aga Khan III (d 1957) overlooks the Nile at Aswan. Appropriately, the building is closely modelled on the Fatimid tombs of Cairo: the Aga Khan, hereditary leader of the world's Ismaili Muslims is reckoned to be the spiritual descendant of the Fatimid Caliphs.

RIGHT *Across the Nile to the west of Aswan, the so-called 'Dome of the Winds' marks the burial place of a venerated medieval* shaykh. *Beneath, the sandstone cliffs are honeycombed with the far older tombs of viceroys, nobles and important officials, some of which date back to Egypt's Old Kingdom period.*

LEFT *Secure on its rocky site above the Nile opposite Aswan, the 7th-century monastery of St Simeon is one of the best-preserved of all early Christian buildings. Once the home of a thriving Coptic community, it was abandoned in the mid-12th century during the conflicts between the Ayyubid dynasty in Cairo and the Nubians to the south.*

Aswan's celebrated Cataract Hotel, built at the turn of the century for the luxury tourist trade, looks out over a passing felucca towards Elephantine Island. The city, once the capital of Southern Egypt, is now a popular winter resort.

RIGHT *Abandoned in the sand in Aswan's ancient Southern Quarry, an unfinished colossus cut from red granite is evidence that Egyptian masons performed at least a basic shaping before a sculpture was moved to its final site. Aswan granite, both abundant and highly prized, was a major source of the town's prosperity.*

LEFT *On the west bank of the Nile near Elephantine Island, an inscribed scale measures the depth of the river. The level of the Nile in flood gave an indication of Egypt's likely prosperity in the coming months, and hence the tax burden its people could bear. This 'Nilometer' was carved in the 7th century* BC.

The ceremonial arcade in Philae's Temple of Isis was erected by the Roman emperors Nero and Tiberius in the 1st century AD, following in a long-established tradition of imperial piety towards Egypt's gods. The original Philae Island was threatened with inundation by the building of the Aswan dam; the Temple of Isis, with Philae's other monuments, was carefully moved to nearby Agilka island.

Its mannered, Roman style contrasting with Philae's more purely Egyptian architecture, the kiosk of the Emperor Trajan overlooks the Nile bank at the Temple of Isis. The kiosk – from a Turkish word denoting an airy pavilion – was originally covered by a spacious, convex roof, now vanished.

LEFT *Under a ceiling decorated with flying vultures, statues of Ramesses II fill the space between floor and ceiling in the interior corridor of the king's rock-cut temple at Abu Simbel. The statues hold the crook and flail that symbolized royal authority.*

RIGHT *From Aswan, the lifeless gravel of the Nubian desert stretches far to the south. Paradoxically, much of the rest of ancient Nubia is now covered by the waters of Lake Nasser behind the Aswan High Dam.*

Modest only in comparison to Abu Simbel's great temple itself, the nearby Temple of Hathor was dedicated to Nofret, principal wife of Ramesses II, as well as to Hathor herself, venerated as the goddess of pleasure and love. Colossal figures of the queen fill the middle niches of the temple front, flanked by those of her all-powerful husband.

A CHRONOLOGY OF EGYPTIAN HISTORY

◆

The division of the rulers of ancient Egypt into dynasties is a legacy of the high priest Manetho, who compiled a history of the kings in the 3rd century BC. Most of his calculations have subsequently been substantiated and form a convenient framework on which to hang the history of Egypt. By contrast, the groupings into kingdoms is a modern scholastic device. Three kingdoms, or periods of stable rule – separated by intermediate periods when the kingdom was fragmented or ruled by invaders – make up the history of Pharaonic Egypt. The Old Kingdom spans the period from the reign of Zoser in the 3rd Dynasty to the collapse of royal authority about 2100 BC. The Middle Kingdom began with the reunification of Upper and Lower Egypt under Mentuhotpe II (2060-2010 BC) and ended with in-fighting among the increasingly powerful governors and nobles. The New Kingdom, the great era of the Egyptian Empire, began with the expulsion of the Asian invaders, the Hyksos, but it too ended in disunity, with Egypt once more under threat from invaders.

Although comparative archaeological, chemical and astronomical dating methods have become increasingly sophisticated and the strenuous efforts of Egyptologists have reduced the margins of error, precise dates for the earlier periods remain elusive. and should be considered approximate. But from the 12th Dynasty they can be accepted with some confidence and with the 26th Dynasty are virtually fixed.

◆

LATE PREDYNASTIC PERIOD (*c* 3150-3050 BC)

Accelerated urbanization at several sites in Egypt; development of hieroglyphic script; possible unification of Egypt.

Scorpion king

◆

ARCHAIC PERIOD (*c* 3050-2695 BC)

1st Dynasty Memphis established as capital; monarchs with the titles Horus (after the god) and Ruler of the Two Lands.

Narmer
Aha } = **Menes?**

2nd Dynasty

Peribsen Uniquely changes title from Horus to Seth.

◆

OLD KINGDOM (*c* 2695-2160 BC)

3rd Dynasty (2695-2575) Zoser First pyramid of stone blocks, built in step form.

4th Dynasty (2575-2465) Era of the great pyramids; appearance of hieratic script.

Sneferu First true pyramid.

Khufu Builder of the great Pyramid at Giza.

Khafre Creator of the Sphinx.

5th Dynasty (2465-2323) Culmination of the cult of Re; erection of sun-temples.

Unas First known appearance of Pyramid Texts.

6th Dynasty (2323-2150)

Pepi I

Pepi II Reported to have reigned 90 years; collapse of royal authority.

7th Dynasty (perhaps non-existent or ephemeral).

8th Dynasty (2150-2134) Direct successors of 6th Dynasty; provincial governors gain autonomy.

FIRST INTERMEDIATE PERIOD (*c* 2134-2040 BC)

9th Dynasty (non-existent or ephemeral governors at Coptos).

10th Dynasty (2134-2040) Direct successors of 8th Dynasty, ruling from Herakleopolis in Lower Egypt.

11th Dynasty Contemporary with 10th Dynasty, ruling from Thebes in Upper Egypt.

Mentuhotpe II (2060-2010) Campaigns against 11th Dynasty and reunites country, leading to 12th Dynasty and Middle Kingdom..

◆

MIDDLE KINGDOM (*c* 2040-1785 BC)

Dates known with some accuracy; introduction of bronze working.

12th Dynasty (2040-1785) Restoration of central power; capital founded at It-Tawi (near Lisht?); promotion of Amun as supreme deity.

Amenemhet I (1991-1962) Conquest of northern Nubia

Senusert III (1878-1844) Suppression of independent governors.

◆

SECOND INTERMEDIATE PERIOD (*c* 1785-1550 BC)

13th Dynasty (1785-1550) Obscure successors of 12th Dynasty. Power exercised by court officials; immigration of south-west Asians into Delta.

14th Dynasty Contemporary with 13th Dynasty. Minor rulers in the Delta.

15th Dynasty (*c* 1640-1555 BC) (Great Hyksos) Throne usurped by the Asian immigrants who establish capital at Avaris; introduction of horses and chariots.

16th Dynasty (Lesser Hyksos) Client princes to the 15th Dynasty.

17th Dynasty (1640-1540) Claim descent from the 12th Dynasty and rule at Thebes. Kamose challenges and expels Hyksos.

◆

NEW KINGDOM (1540-1070 BC)

The Egyptian Empire

18th Dynasty (1540-1307) Direct descendants of the 17th Dynasty. A period of great expansion into south-west Asia and Nubia; Thebes developed into vast ceremonial city.

Amenhotpe I (1525-1504)

Tuthmosis I (1504-1492)

Hatshepsut (1473-1458) Queen co-ruling with Tuthmosis.

Tuthmosis III (1479-1425) Co-ruler with Hatshepsut; after her death attempts to erase her memory.

Amenhotpe III (1391-1353)

Amenhotpe IV (Akhenaten) (1353-1335) Abandons Thebes and worship of Amun; founds new city Akhetaten for adoration of the Aten.

Tutankhamun (1333-1323) Re-establishment of the worship of Amun.

19th Dynasty (1307-1196) Founded by military commander, Ramesses I. Increasing belligerence of Libyans and south-west Asians.

Seti I (1306-1290)

Ramesses II (1290-1224) Phenomenal building programme including temple at Abu Simbel; transfers capital to Per-Ramesse in Delta.

Merenptah (1236-1223) Possibly the period of the Biblical Exodus.

20th Dynasty (1196-1070) Founded by Sethnakhte. Rise to prominence of High Priests of Amun at Thebes; Libyan mercenaries settled in the Delta.

Ramesses III (1194-1163) Most capable king, followed by several descendants.

Ramesses XI (1099-1069) Divides rule with Viceroy of Kush and High Priest of Amun.

◆

THIRD INTERMEDIATE PERIOD (*c* 1069-525 BC)

21st Dynasty (1069-945) Country divided between kings at Tanis (in the Delta) and related High Priests of Amun at Thebes.

Smendes I (1060-1043) at Tanis: Pinudjem I (1070-1055) at Thebes.

Pseusennes I (1039-991) at Tanis: Menkheperre (1045-992) at Thebes.

22nd Dynasty (945-712) Monarchy at Tanis and high priestship pass to settled Libyans.

Shoshenk I (945-924) Daughter married to Hebrew King Solomon.

Osorkon II (*c* 883-855)

Takeloth II (850-825)

23rd Dynasty (828-712) Parallel with 22nd Dynasty established at Leontopolis.

24th Dynasty (724-712) as 23rd Dynasty but based at Sais.

25th Dynasty (712-656) Nubians from Napata wishing to reimpose order in Egypt, by now disintegrated into several distinct states; introduction of iron working.

Shabaka (712-698) Rule from Memphis.

Taharqa (690-664) Invasion of Assyrians; Memphis and Thebes sacked; foundation of Babylon of Egypt, south of Heliopolis.

26th Dynasty (664-525) Nubians, originating at Sais, assume control with the assistance of Greek mercenaries.

Psamtik I (664-610) Increasing Greek presence in Egypt.

Neko II (610-595) Attempts to build canal in Delta between Nile and Red Sea.Circumnavigation of Africa?

Amasis (570-526) Last great pharaoh of Egypt; Greeks settled at Naukratis.

◆

LATE PERIOD (*c* 525-332 BC)

27th Dynasty (525-404) Occupation by Persians, who assume royal titles

Cambyses (525-521)

Darius I (521-485) Completes Red Sea Canal of Neko I

Artaxerxes I (464-423) The Greek historian Herodotus in Egypt *c*453.

28th Dynasty (404-399) Expulsion of Persians, brief reign of Amyrteos of Sais.

29th Dynasty (399-380) Four kings originating from Mendes.

30th Dynasty (380-341) Several kings from Sebennytos.

Nekhtnebef I (380-362)

31st Dynasty) (343-332) Second Persian occupation.

Darius III (335-332) Represses an intrusive revolt by the last native king, Kababash; Darius defeated in Persia by Alexander the Great.

◆

MACEDONIAN PERIOD (332-305 BC)

Alexander the Great (332-323) Accepted as legitimate king; foundation of Alexandria.

◆

PTOLEMAIC PERIOD (305-30 BC)

Ptolemy I Soter (305-283) Commander of Alexander. Foundation of Museum and Library of Alexandria; Promotion of the cult of Sarapis

Ptolemy II Philadelphus (285-246) Construction of the Pharos (great lighthouse) at Alexandria.

Ptolemy VII Euergetes (163-116)

Cleopatra VII (51-30) Alliances with brothers Ptolemies XII and XIII, Julius Caesar and Mark Antony; her army defeated by Octavian, who executes Ptolemy XIV Caesarion, son of Cleopatra and Caesar; Egypt a Roman province.

◆

ROMAN PERIOD (30 BC – AD 395)

Equestrian prefects imposed as governors.

Trajan (98-117) Builds canal from Babylon of Egypt to join Delta canal to Red Sea.

Hadrian (117-138) Tours Egypt twice; founds Antinopolis.

Marcus Aurelius (161-180) Catechitical School founded at Alexandria.

Septimius Severus (193-211) First persecution of Christians in Egypt.

270 Beginning of monastic movement.

Diocletian (284-305) Great Persecution of the Christians; start of the Coptic calendar.

Constantine (306-337) Edict of Milan, persecution of Christians halted; Pachomius founds the first monastery.

Theodosius I (379-395) Last known hieroglyphic inscriptions.

◆

BYZANTINE PERIOD (AD 395-640)

Division of Roman Empire into East and West, with Egypt ruled from Constantinople.

Theodosius II (408-450) Widespread destruction of pagan temples by clergy. Lady Hypatia murdered in Alexandria.

Marcian (450-457) After Council of Chalcedon, Egyptian church splits away from rest of Christian community.

Justinian (527-565) Harassment of Coptic Christians by Byzantines; last pagan temples closed in Egypt; Christianization of Nubia.

Heraclius (610-641) Persian occupation (617-628); persecution of Coptic Christians by Patriarch Cyrus.

◆

MUSLIM PERIOD (AD 640-)

Conquest of Egypt by Amr ibn al-As for Khalif Umar; founds capital Fustat at Babylon of Egypt; builds first mosque in Africa; introduction of Islamic calendar.

Umayyad Khalifs (658-750) at Damascus. Appoint governors for Egypt.

Arabic introduced as official language in 704.

Abbasid Khalifs (750-868) at Baghdad. Continue to appoint governors.

Tulunids (868-905)

Ahmad ibn Tulun (868-884) Achieves independence in Egypt and Syria; builds new city north of Fustat.

Abbasid Khalifs (905-925) Reimpose authority.

Ikhshids (935-969) Autonomous with approval of Abbasids.

Muhammad ibn Tughj (925-946)

Kafur (966-968) true ruler since death of Ibn Tughj.

Fatimid Khalifs (969-1171) Ismail Shiah from Tunisia. Capture Egypt and establish Khalifate in direct opposition to Abbasids at Baghdad.

al-Muizz (969-975) Builds city of al-Qahirah north of Fustat.

al-Hakim (996-1021) Of mercurial nature, he announces his divinity and disappears.

al-Mustali (1094-1101) Leadership of Ismails passes to Assassins.

Ayyubids (1171-1251)

Salah al-Din [Saladin] (1171-1193) Assumes power with title of sultan after death of last Fatimid Khalif; return of Egypt from Shiite to Sunni Islam; Cairo refortified.

al-Kamil (1218-1238) Crusaders occupy Damietta; St Francis of Assisi visits sultan.

al-Salih Ayyub (1240-1249) Second Crusader invasion; King Louis IX of France captured and ransomed.

Bahri Mamelukes (1250-1382) Military slaves (*mamluk*) of the Ayyubids assume power.

Shajar al-Durr (1250) Wife of al-Salih Ayyub and only female sultan.

Baybars (1260-1277) Defeats advancing Mongols and begins expansion of Mameluke state into Syria; Seat of Abbasid Khalifate set up in Cairo.

Khalil (1290-94) Final expulsion of Crusaders from Middle East.

al-Nasir Muhammad (1294-1340 with two usurpations).

Burgi Mamelukes (1382-1517)

Muayyad Shaykh (1412-1421) Mameluke state reaches greatest extent.

Barsbay (1422-1437) Cyprus tributary to Egypt; growing truculence of Mameluke troops.

Qayt-bay (1468-1496) Pinnacle of late Mameluke art; Mameluke soldiers almost uncontrollable.

Qansuh al-Ghawri (1501-1517) Portuguese establish sea route to India; Mameluke army defeated by the Ottoman Sultan Selim in Syria; Egypt becomes province again.

◆

OTTOMAN PERIOD (1517-1914)

Governors imposed from Istanbul.

1650s Increasing autonomy of the local Mameluke beys (grandees).

1700s last use of Coptic as living language.

Ali Bey al-Kabir (1760-1772) Accepted by Ottoman sultan as ruler of Egypt.

French Occupation (1798-1801) Bonaparte defeats Beys and undertakes extensive survey of Egypt; French expelled by combined Ottoman and British armies.

Khedives (1805-1953) Wholesale introduction of European methods and ideas; occupation of Sudan.

Muhammad Ali Pasha (1805-1848) Gains acceptance for hereditary right of governorship of Egypt.

1810-22 Publication of the *Description de l'Egypte*, the results of French survey.

1818 Champollion deciphers the hieroglyphics on Rosetta Stone.

Ismail (1868-1879) Increasing indebtedness to European bankers.

1865 Thomas Cook organizes regular tours of Egypt.

1869 Opening of Suez Canal.

Muhammad Tawfiq (1879-1892)

1882 Bombardment of Alexandria and British occupation.

Abbas II (1892-1914)

1914 Abbas deposed; Egypt made independent of Turkey.

Ahmad Fuad (1917-1936)

1922 Kingdom founded; discovery of Tomb of Tutankhamun by Howard Carter.

Faruq (1936-1952)

1942 Western desert campaign of Second World War

1952 Sudan gains independence; Faruq deposed by Organization of Free Officers.

◆

REPUBLIC (1953-)

Gamal Abd al-Nasser (1953-1970)

1953 Agricultural Reform Act, large estates redistributed among farmers.

1954 Evacuation of British troops from Egypt.

1956 Abortive attempt at occupation of Canal Zone by Britain, France and Israel.

1970 Opening of the High Dam at Aswan.

◆

A GUIDE TO EGYPTIAN DEITIES

◆

The myths of Egypt were developed over a period of three thousand years, time enough for them to be obscured under layers of creative literary invention by generations of scribes and priests. Even the late third millenium BC Pyramid Texts had had nearly a thousand years in which to mature, while later texts, supposedly copied from ancient sources, may well have been deliberately written in an archaic style to give them a desired venerability, a practice at which the scribes were extremely adept. Aspects of myths could be promoted or suppressed or new motifs introduced if they harmonized with the whole. Gods could be supplicated in one aspect or many, and new gods could be constructed from the epithets of earlier deities, while they in turn could be assimilated by more powerful gods.

◆

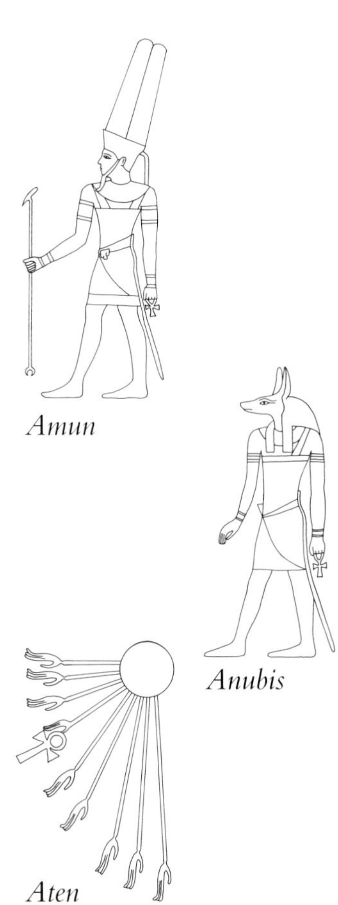

Amun

Anubis

Aten

AMUN

From the Middle Kingdom considered the supreme god and patron of the pharaohs, with cult centre at Thebes. Amun sometimes assumed the properties of other gods when he was known as Amun-Re, Amun-Min etc. He is usually shown in a kilt and a crown with two tall plumes or with a ram's head, and often with blue skin, the colour of sacred lapis lazuli.

ANUBIS

The patron god of the cemetery and funerary rites. He was supposed to have invented embalming, which he first practised on the corpse of Osiris. One of his particular functions was the weighing of the heart of the deceased. He is depicted as a reclining jackal or man with a jackal's head.

ATEN

'Father and mother of all creation', Aten is always portrayed as the sun disk, with radiating beams ending in small hands. Akhenaten (18th Dynasty) promoted the cult of Aten and worshipped him to the exclusion of almost all other deities, building a new cult centre at Tell el-Amarna.

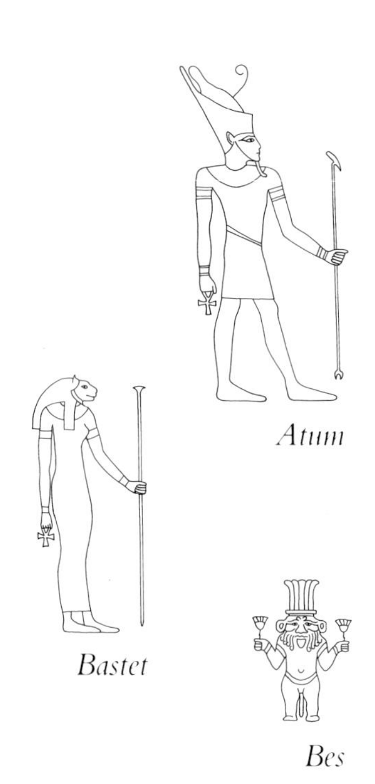

Atum

Bastet

Bes

ATUM

One of the solar gods of Heliopolis, often identified with the setting sun. A creator god, in a strange early concept he is considered self-engendered. He wears the double crown and carries a staff of office. A bull known as the Mnervis which was kept at the temple was regarded as his living aspect.

BASTET

Originally an avenging lioness deity, her ferocious traits were later suppressed and she was worshipped as a peaceful cat. Her cult centre was at Bubastis in the western Delta, where there was an immense cemetery for mummified cats.

BES

A grotesque dwarf, associated with childbirth and children, and also with entertainment. Unlike the other gods, he is always represented full faced rather than in profile, usually with a large crown of feathers on his head.

GEB, NUT and SHU

Geb, Nut his sister and wife, and Shu their father form an elemental group. Shu, god of light and air, fathered the children by Tefnut, goddess of moisture. Geb, the earth god, is depicted reclining on the ground with Nut, goddess of the sky, arching over him while Shu, in human form with an ostrich plume on his head, holds them apart. (Geb and Nut can also appear in isolation: Geb wearing on his head the hieroglyph of his name and his symbol, the goose, and Nut as the celestial cow.) In one mythic cycle Nut gave birth to Osiris and his brothers and sisters; in another, she swallows the sun each night and gives birth to him each morning. She also has a funerary function and is often painted inside coffin lids.

Geb, Nut and Shu

Hapy *Hathor* *Horus* *Isis*

HAPY

God of the Nile inundation, represented as a podgy man with a plume of Nile plants. He often appears in dual form, with one twin wearing the papyrus of Upper Egypt and the other the water lily of Lower Egypt.

HATHOR

A cow goddess, associated with festivity and love, and worshipped as protector of the ruler and the dead. Her centres were at Denderah, and, with Horus, at Edfu, at both of which she was considered as Horus' consort. She is depicted as a woman with the sun's disk between horns or as a cow.

HORUS

The falcon god, epitome of divine kingship from the earliest time. An extremely complex deity appearing in many aspects: as a child, son of Osiris and Isis, opponent of Seth and a sun god. The reigning pharaoh was regarded as an incarnation of Horus. The falcon was a powerful image for the ancient Egyptians; several other gods were depicted in this form.

ISIS

One of the most important of goddesses. As consort of the murdered Osiris, she was associated with mourning and funeral rites; as mother of Horus, she was a life-giver and protector of the ruler; most importantly, as the enchantress who had brought Osiris back to life, she was a healer. She is shown as a woman with her symbol, a throne, on her head, sometimes holding the infant Horus.

Khephri *Khnum* *Khonsu*

KHEPHRI

A solar god of Heliopolis and a symbol of rebirth. He represents the rising sun and is depicted in the form of a scarab beetle, whose life cycle was seen as parallel to the daily rebirth of the sun.

KHNUM

God of the cataracts and a creator. His centre was at Aswan where he formed a triad with the goddesses Satet and Anket. He is portrayed as a ram-headed man.

KHONSU

A moon god. Originally a spirit-companion of the ruler in hunting aggressive gods, he was later considered son of Amun and Mut with whom he formed the triad of Thebes. On his head is a combination of the crescent and full moon.

Maat
Min
Montu
Mut
Nefertum
Neith
Nekhbet

MAAT

Symbol of universal stability, associated with justice, order, righteousness and truth. Maat was the daughter of Re and consort of Thoth. She was essential to the existence of all other gods and only her support gave legitimacy to the king's rule. She is shown as a woman wearing an ostrich plume.

MIN

The personification of fertility and sexual procreation, because of which his attributes were often assumed by other deities. His main centres were at Akhmin and Qift. He is depicted as a mummiform figure with erect penis, wearing a crown with two tall plumes and holding a flail.

MONTU

The war god of Hermonthis (now Armant, near Luxor), shown as a falcon-headed man. He had several sanctuaries in the Theban area and his own precinct at Karnak. The Bucchis bull was his living aspect.

MUT

Consort of Amun, protector of the pharaoh, and mother of Khonsu. Like Amun she also assimilated the characteristics of other deities, such as Isis, Sakhmet etc. She is depicted with feathered dress and vulture-skin head-dress. wearing the double crown of Upper and Lower Egypt.

NEFERTUM

The personification of the primaeval blue water lily which in his portrayals he wears on his head. Son of Ptah and Sakhmet, the other members of the triad of Memphis. He was also important at the sanctuaries of Bastet and Wadjet in the Delta.

NEITH

Goddess of Sais in Lower Egypt. A creator goddess, she is shown wearing the red crown of Lower Egypt or her symbol and hieroglyph, a shield and crossed arrows. Because of this she is associated with the military victories of the ruler.

NEKHBET (Nekhebet)

Vulture goddess of el-Kab in southern Egypt and protectress of rulers. She is depicted as a woman or in the form of a vulture spreading her wings over the Pharaoh, and as the head of a vulture she appears next to Wadjet on the king's diadem.

NEPHTHYS

Consort of Seth and sister of Isis, protector of the ruler and associated with funerary rites. She helped Isis in the search for Osiris' body. She is depicted with her symbol, a mansion, on her head.

Nephthys

NUT *See* GEB, NUT and SHU

OSIRIS

One of the most important gods; judge of the dead, ruler of the afterworld and personification of the dead. He was supposed to have been murdered by Seth and brought to life by Isis, after which he remained in the underworld. One of his principal centres was Abydos. He is shown as a mummiform figure with a white crown and two plumes, holding a crook and flail.

Osiris

PTAH

Principal god of Memphis, a creator deity and the patron of craftsmen. He is shown as mummiform figure wearing a blue skull cap and holding a *djed* staff, the emblem of life. The Apis bull of Memphis was his living manifestation.

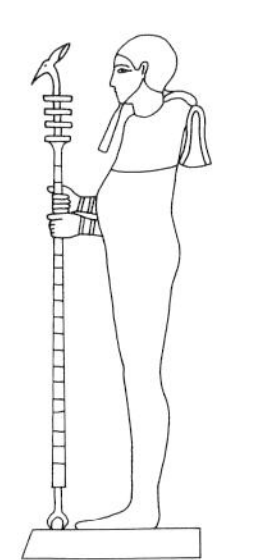

Ptah

RE

One of the most important gods; god of the sun and of creation. He was supposed to travel across the sky in his boat each day, and through the underworld in another boat each night, where he defeated the agents of chaos. He is depicted as a man with a falcon head above which is the disk of the sun.

Re

SAKHMET

Lion goddess of war. The consort of Ptah and mother of Nefertum, she was the second member of the triad of Memphis. She is depicted as a woman with a lion's head, above which is the disk of the sun. She also has a healing aspect.

Sakhmet

SARAPIS

The personification of the dead Apis bull as Osiris, a deity promoted by Ptolemy I. A god of the underworld and fertility, his largest temple was at Alexandria. He assumed the aspects of several Greek gods and is always shown in hellenistic form as a vigorous bearded man, often with a corn measure crown.

Sarapis

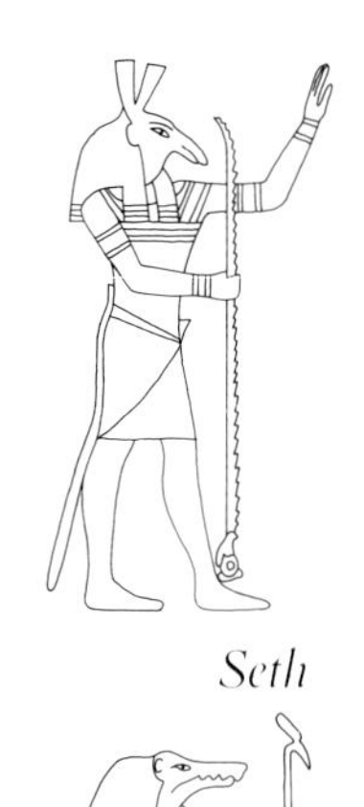

Seth

SETH

A god of equivocal character, associated with the desert and forces of disruption. He could appear in evil or beneficial aspects, in contention or harmony with Horus, and was accordingly despised or venerated. Seth was believed to be the brother or the son of Osiris, and during the late pharaonic period was regarded as his murderer. His form is that of the strange 'Seth animal', with slanting eyes and square-tipped ears, or its head on a human body.

SHU *See* GEB, NUT and SHU

Sobek

SOBEK

Crocodile god, seen in his animal shape or as a man with crocodile head. He was particularly venerated in the Fayyum – where live sacred crocodiles were kept at his sanctuaries – and with Horus at Kom Ombo.He may have been associated with death and burial, later becoming a patron of kings.

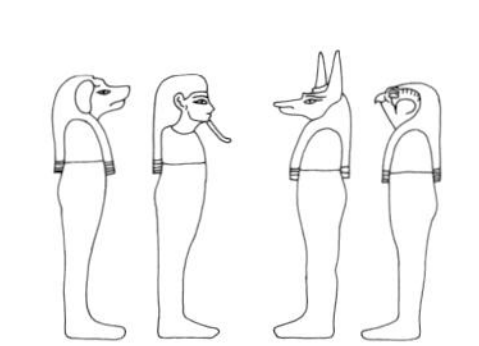

Sons of Horus

SONS OF HORUS

Four mummiform gods protecting the entrails of the deceased: Imsety, a man (liver); Hapy, a baboon (lungs); Duamutef, a jackal (stomach); and Qebehsenuf, a falcon (intestines). Their heads often capped the canopic jars, in which the entrails were kept.

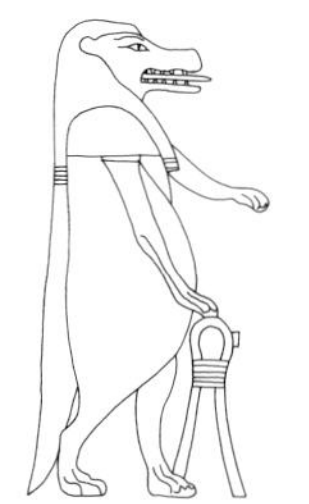

Tawaret

TAWARET

Goddess of childbirth and consort of Amun. her temple was near the great temple of Amun-Re at Karnak. She is depicted as a bipedal hippopotamus holding the *sa* symbol of protection. Like Bes she was the object of a popular cult among the populace.

Thoth

THOTH

The moon god, patron of scribes and thus knowledge; he was believed to have invented writing and scribes were called disciples of Thoth. His main centre was at Ashmunayn (Hermopolis). Thoth appears as a baboon or ibis or an ibis-headed man.

Wadjet

WADJET

Cobra goddess of Buto in the Delta, defender of the ruler and tutelary deity of Lower Egypt. She appears in the form of a serpent on the ruler's head-dress next to Nekhbet and accompanies her in the Two Ladies title of the King.

◆

A GUIDE TO HIEROGLYPHS AND SYMBOLS

◆

The language of ancient Egypt was one of the Afro-Asiatic group related to modern Arabic, Hebrew and Ethiopic, but closer to Berber and Nubian. However, the remarkable script developed about 3000 BC seems to have been an indigenous development;.the Egyptians themselves attributed its invention to the god Thoth. Hieroglyphs (from the Greek words *hieros,* and 'sacred' and *gluphikos* 'carving') were suitable only for decorative monumental writing, and are found mainly on the walls of temples and tombs.

Probably stimulated by the burgeoning bureaucracy in the 4th Dynasty (about 2500 years BC, a cursive form of writing (i.e. with simplified characters) known as *hieratic* ('priestly') emerged, suitable for writing on papyrus scrolls with ink. While hieroglyphs continued to be used until about the 3rd century AD, the hieratic script was much more commonly used, mainly for religious documents. In about the 7th century BC hieratic script gave way to an even more economical cursive script, *demotic* ('popular'), which was used in ordinary official documents. The use of hieroglyphs persisted as late as the Ptolemaic period, when its association with the traditional religion gave it a particular emotional significance for the Egyptians under foreign rule. With the arrival of Christianity in Egypt in the 2nd century AD, the use of the ancient scripts declined very rapidly. Egyptian Christians used the Greek alphabet, adding seven demotic signs to represent sounds not available in the Greek script. The last known example of hieroglyphs is a rock inscription on the island of Philae, which dates from 394.

Once the hieroglyphic script fell out of use, the secret of its meaning was quickly lost. Attempts through the ages to decipher it failed because most people believed it was a system of symbols rather than an alphabet. It was not until the 19th century that the code was finally broken. In 1799, at a town called Rashid (Rosetta), members of Napoleon's expedition to Egypt discovered a stone bearing inscriptions in Greek, hieroglyphic and demotic script. The Greek writing stated that the stone bore the same text set out in all three languages. Several scholars attempted to decipher the hieroglyphs on what became known as the Rosetta Stone, and in 1818 the Frenchman Jean-François Champollion (1790-1832) finally succeeded.

◆

Symbols used in the hieroglyphic script were drawn from many sources: animals, plants, the physical universe, humans and their occupations, buildings and furniture. Some examples are given below.

Hieroglyphs can be divided into three categories: ideograms, which were simply pictures of the things they referred to; phonograms, which represented the sound of the thing depicted, but could refer to something else with a similar sound; and determinatives, which were not pronounced, but served to reinforce the meaning of a group of symbols, usually to avoid confusion. Many symbols could have any of these functions according to context. The whole language was governed by a strict grammatical code, with plurals indicated by three vertical strokes. As in related languages, and to the despair of modern scholars, vowels were not indicated but understood.

IDEOGRAMS

Simple picture symbols, pronounced as the name of what they represent. They were distinguished by an accompanying stroke.

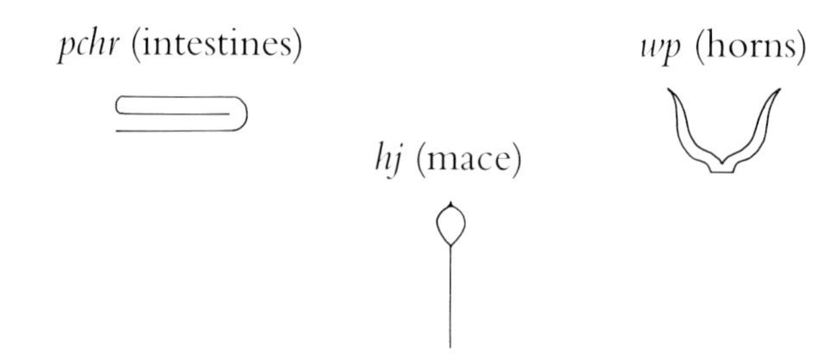

PHONOGRAMS

These represented not the thing they depicted, but the sound of its name. Thus the symbol for *ht*, a branch, could be used for the sound *ht* occurring in any other word. There were about 100 signs used for forming words phonetically, and these are further divisible according to the number of their consonants. The most common were *uniliterals*, 24 signs each representing a single sound. They constitute all the sounds used in the language and are often equated with an alphabet. (see chart opposite.) One or more unpronounced unilaterals often followed a word to reiterate its pronounciation.

UNILITERAL CONSONANTS *(Alphabet)*

Where no explanation of sound is given it is approximately as in English. The transliteration is not scholarly but designed to allow easier recognition. Note there is no 'L'.

SIGN	SOUND	TRANSLITERATION	SIGN	SOUND	TRANSLITERATION
	a as in apple	*a*		ch as in loch	*kh*
	ee as in feet	*y* or *i*		ch as in German ich	*x*
	glottal sound*	'	 *or*	s	*s*
 *or* 	oo as in boot	*w* or *u*		sh as in shop	*sh*
	b	*b*		k (emphatic)	*q*
	p	*p*		k	*k*
	f	*f*		g (hard)	*g*
 *or* 	m	*m*		t	*t*
or 	n	*n*		ch as in chat	*ch*
	r	*r*		d	*d*
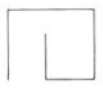	h	*h*		j	*j*
	h (emphatic)	*h*	 *or* 	ee as in feet	*y* or *i*

* now used only in Semitic languages.

Biliterals and *triliterals* were signs representing a combination of two and three sounds respectively, e.g.

Some quadrilaterals were also used.

DETERMINATIVES

These were auxiliary signs placed after a word to clarify or emphasize its meaning, but not pronounced. They could be *generic*, denoting action or motion, for instance, or *specific*, like the signs for sky, wall etc.

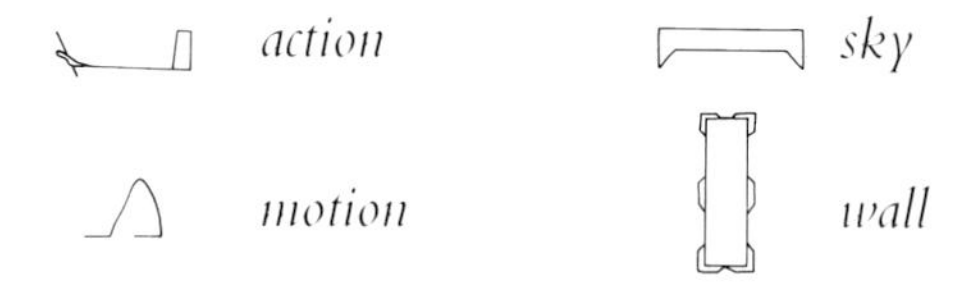

Some signs could fulfil any of these functions according to context. For instance, the sign for the trilateral *khnt* shown above could also appear as an ideogram meaning nose or upper face, or it could be a determinative, indicating that the word it accompanied had something to do with noses, smelling, breathing, sneezing etc.

Hieroglyphs can be read from right to left, left to right or downwards (never upwards) The direction is indicated by the front of faces or objects, which face towards the beginning of the line, with the upper signs always read first. However, in all periods symbols with royal or religious significance were placed first, regardless of sense. In the absence of vowels it is impossible to reconstruct the pronunciation of the ancient language and therefore scholars arbitrarily insert the letter 'e' after consonants to make the text readable.

The example below shows how the system actually worked. It contains examples of most of the above forms and is taken from an ostrich feather fan of Tutankhamun. Most of the numbered elements use both spoken and unspoken signs; 5, 7 and 8 use only phonograms, while 10 uses only an ideogram. The bracketed part of the explanation refers to the grey shaded areas.

comp: complementary phonogram gen: generic determinative id: ideogram phon: phonograms pl: plural s: specific determinative

1	*b-h-t* ph (sp fan)	FAN	8	*m* ph	WHEN
2	*shu-t* ph (comp *u*) (pl)	FEATHERS	9	*b-h-s-u* ph (gen action)	HUNTING
3	*n-`u* (pl, sp ostrich)	OSTRICHES	10	*hr* id	UPON
4	*in* ph (comp *n*)	OBTAINED	11	*khst* id (comp *t*) (line for id)	DESERT
5	*n* ph	BY	12	*yabtt* id (comp. *btt*) (sp alien place)	EAST
6	*hm* ph (sp king)	MAJESTY	13	*yun-nu* ph (sp town)	YUNU (i.e.
7	*f* ph	HIS			Heliopolis).

1 2 3 4 5 6 7 8 9 10 11 12 13

Thus it reads 'The fan ostrich feathers obtained by his majesty when hunting in the desert east of Heliopolis.'

One of the most frequent hieroglyphic formulae was the titulary of the ruler, the five great names, which although varied in themselves were always introduced by specific titles. The first two predate the dynastic period but the sequence was fixed by the 5th Dynasty and remained unchanged until the Roman period.

This titulary of Nekhtnebef I, shown below, is a late example and demonstrates the persistence of tradition over a vast period of time. Note that the birds are facing right, so the symbols are read from right to left, and each group from top to bottom. The sequence of names is as follows:

1 **Horus** the most ancient element which always takes precedence. **Chema** 'The vigorous'.
2 **Two ladies** (*nubti*) The goddesses Nekhbet of Upper Egypt and Wadjet of Lower Egypt who protect the ruler. **Semnekh tawi** 'Who reorganizes the two lands'
3 **Golden Horu** an obscure title. **Ir meret netchru** 'Who does as the gods wish'.
4 **Sedge and the Bee** (*nesu bit*) This emphasized the Pharaoh's rule over Upper (sedge) and Lower (Bee) Egypt. It always refers to the god Re. **Kheper ka re** 'Spirit of Re reborn' (the sun-disk is Re's symbol).
5 **Son of Re** (*Sa re*) **'Nekht-neb-ef'** The Pharaoh's own birth-name, the one by which he is generally known.

The last two names are always placed within a cartouche. This originally represented a rope; it signified eternity, and was also supposed to protect the owner of the name from harm.

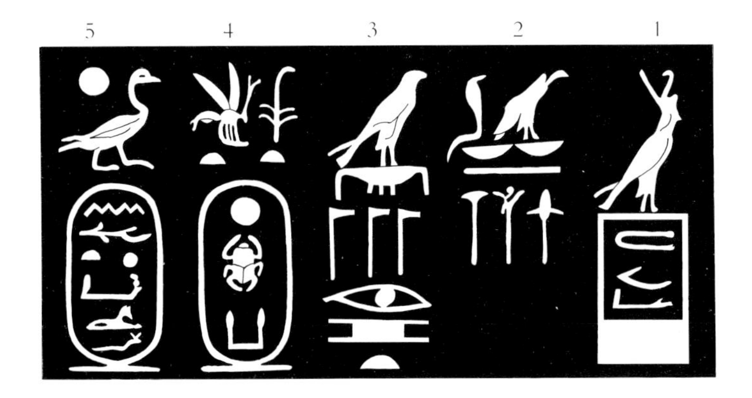

◆

GLOSSARY OF ARCHITECTURAL TERMS

Ambon Pulpit in a Coptic church.

Basilica An early form of church, divided into a nave and two or more aisles based on plan of Byzantine court. It evolved from the Roman basilica, which was a large meeting-hall.

Cult temple A temple built for the worship of the local deity. These are found mainly on sites of extreme antiquity.

Deir Arabic term for monastery.

Haykal screen The partition separating the apse from the nave in a Coptic Church.

Hypostyle hall The first, pillared and roofed chamber beyond the portal of an ancient temple.

Madrasah A Muslim religious college, introduced in Ayyubid times for the encouragement of Sunni theology. The architecture was influenced by domestic palaces. In the Mameluke period madrasahs assumed a cruciform plan which influenced mosque design and eventually supplanted the enclosure format.

Mammisi A word invented by Champollion (see p.28) to describe the kiosks in temple precincts. Mammisi were used to celebrate the birth mysteries of the god of the temple.

Mihrab A niche in the wall of a mosque facing Mecca, in front of which the *imam* (prayer leader) stands.

Minaret (Arabic *manarah*, *madhanah*) A tall structure attached to a mosque from which the call to prayer is made. Early examples are in the form of square towers but in the Mameluke period they evolved into three-tiered buildings and in Ottoman times became slender and round with pointed tops.

Minbar The stepped 'chair' in a mosque to the right of the *mihrab* from which the Friday *khutbah* (sermon) is read.

Mortuary temple A temple used in the cult of the dead king. Mortuary temples were riginally attached to the ruler's pyramid, but later were built away from the tomb, although still in the same general area.

Naos The stone or wooden shrine in the sanctuary of a temple in which the image of the god was kept.

Narthex A transverse porch in a Coptic church.

Pylon Vast tapered towers either side of the portal of an ancient temple.

Sanctuary The innermost room of an ancient temple, the 'holy of holies'.

State temple A temple built by the ruler ostensibly for the gods but in fact for his own glorification, as at Karnak and Memphis.

Valley temple A temple connected to the mortuary temple by a causeway. Like mortuary temples they were originally built next to the ruler's pyramid, but later examples are displaced from the actual tomb.

FURTHER READING

◆

Most of the books listed here are widely available, but a few are included because they are the only ones to deal with a specific subject; for instance, no-one has attempted a single-volume chronological history of Egypt since 1904. Most titles include more specialized bibliographies.

Abu Lughod, Janet L. *Cairo: 1001 Years of the City Victorious* (Princeton University Press, Princeton, NJ, 1971)

Amherst, Lady *A Sketch of Egyptian History from the Earliest Times to the Present Day.* (Methuen, London, 1904)

Badawy, Alexander *Coptic Art and Archaeology* (MIT Press, Cambridge, MA, 1978)

Baines, J. and Malek, J.*Encyclopaedia of Ancient Egypt* (Phaidon, London, 1980)

Bowman, Alan K. *Egypt after the Pharoahs* (British Museum Publications, London, 1986)

Gardiner, Sir A. *Egyptian Grammar* (Oxford University Press, Oxford, many editions)

Glanville, S. R. K. *The Legacy of Egypt* (Oxford University Press, Oxford, 1942; reprinted)

Hart, G. *A Dictionary of Egyptian Gods and Goddesses* (Penguin, Harmondsworth, 1986)

Herodotus *The Histories*, translated by Aubry de Sélincourt (Penguin, Harmondsworth,1972)

Holt, P. M *The Age of the Crusades* (Longman, London, 1986)

Holt, P. M. *Egypt and the Fertile Crescent* 1516-1922 (Cornell University Press, Ithaca, NY, 1980)

James, T. G. H. *An Introduction to Ancient Egyp*t (British Museum Publications, 1979; reprinted)

Kemp, B. *Egypt: Anatomy of a Civilisation* (Routledge, London, 1989)

Lane-Poole *A History of Egypt in the Middle Ages* (Methuen, London, 1901)

El-Masri, I. H. *The Story of the Copts* (Middle East Council of Churches, Cairo, ?1986)

Smith, W. Stevenson *The Art and Architecture of Ancient Egypt* (Penguin, Harmondsworth, 1981)

Seton-Williams, V. and Stocks, P. *Egypt: Blue Guide* (A. & C. Black, London, 1989)

Wilkinson, R. *Reading Egyptian Art* (Thames and Hudson, London, 1992)

◆

INDEX

◆

◆